Learning to teach reading

Learning to teach reading

Geoffrey R. Roberts

P·C·P
Paul Chapman
Publishing Ltd

Acknowledgements

The author would like to thank Tegwen Roberts for advice on children's use of language and on textual matters. The author and publishers would like to thank David Griffiths for the photograph of Judith Piotrowski and her children, Jennifer and Richard, on page 2, (Figure 1.1) and for the photographs on pages 23 (Figure 2.1), 30 (Figure 2.3), 36 (Figure 2.6) and 79 (Figure 3.2); the headteachers, staff and children of Vernon Park Primary School, Stockport and of Medlock Primary School, Manchester for the photographs on pages 24 (Figure 2.2) and 55 (Figure 3.1), and Miss Roni Armstrong for the work sheets on pages 32 and 33.

© Copyright 1999 Geoffrey R. Roberts

First published 1999

Paul Chapman Publishing Ltd
A SAGE Publications Company
6 Bonhill Street
London EC2A 4PU

SAGE Publications Inc
2455 Teller Road
Thousand Oaks, California 91320

SAGE Publications India Pvt Ltd
32, M-Block Market
Greater Kailash – I
New Delhi 110 048

British Library Cataloguing in Publication data

A catalogue record for this book is available from the British Library

ISBN 0 7619 6328 6
ISBN 0 7619 6329 4 (pbk)

Library of Congress catalog card number available

Typeset by Anneset Ltd, Weston-super-Mare, Somerset
Printed and bound in Great Britain

Contents

Proficient reading depends on an automatic capacity to recognise frequent spelling patterns visually and to translate them phonologically . . . The issue is how best to couch phonic instruction, how to build to it, from it, and around it in ways that best ensure the ease and productivity of its acquisition. The issue is how to make instruction on word recognition skills a self-engendering, motivating, and meaningful experience for the students [pupils] and a manageable one for their teachers.

M. J. Adams, 1992

Preface

This book attempts to do four things. First it outlines the process of learning to read and the implications of this for teachers. The view is taken that teaching children to read involves teaching reading behaviours which enable children to use the facts that are learned and the skills that are acquired. These behaviours include spelling and writing as well as the adoption of searching and flexible strategies to facilitate the associating of print with language and thought. In the second place, responses to some basic considerations are offered. These cover issues which face all teachers of young children before they can determine a programme that suits both them and the children. Thirdly, a programme is outlined that covers teaching children to read and suggests ways in which spelling and writing may contribute to the task. This programme includes both the learning that is necessary and the teaching that enables it to be accomplished. It goes further than the statement from Adams on the previous page in proposing that phonics, although an essential and important ingredient in learning to read, is by no means the only issue confronting those who teach children to read. Finally, the allocation of one hour per day or its equivalent to the development of literacy is placed within a model of teaching that is practical to implement and theoretically sound.

Geoffrey R. Roberts
The Centre for Primary Education
University of Manchester

1 Learning to read

It is a peculiarity of the topic of learning to read that although it receives a great deal of attention in the press and especially amongst politicians, these same interested people tend to fall into the trap of giving the impression that teaching a child to read is a simple matter, requiring only a little diligence on the part of teachers. Perhaps it is the result of teachers being so successful, for in truth the degree of success that is involved in ensuring such a high degree of literacy amongst the adult population is a tribute to our schools.

Nevertheless, success should not blind us to the fact that the acquisition of skill in reading is a highly complex matter. It depends upon a substantial amount of preparatory work in which children begin to become aware of the nature of print, to realise that it conveys a message and that it is possible to interpret that message. This means that at a very early age, when, as Piaget has shown, children's mental activities are severely constrained in terms of dealing with abstract matters, they have to begin to understand something of the nature of texts, firstly that they can make responses to texts in terms of sounds which are attached to symbols and, secondly, that texts have a form and structure which affects their meaning.

If one thinks about these two things it will soon become obvious that each embraces many sub-skills: all of those which contribute to the identification of unknown words and all of those which enable a reader to interpret words in a text. Obviously, these skills only develop over a prolonged period of time, frequently beginning in the home where the child is read to every day and where the parent makes constant references to print in the environment – labels on containers in the kitchen, shop and road signs, street names and the print of favourite story books. This gradual induction into the world of print under the attentive eye of a parent is crucial and something that schools find difficult to compensate for when it is missing from the homes of less fortunate children. Where better to learn the procedures of

1

reading a book, if not the details, than with a parent who is reading for the child's pleasure? In the warmth and security of this position, with no question of being tested or challenged, children can discover how adults hold the book, where they begin and where their eyes are looking. They can enjoy the repetition of favourite stories and so can both repeatedly meet words that thus become visually familiar and experience language and structures that are new to them (Figure 1.1).

The contrast between the prolonged period of preparation that some children get in the home and the difficulties of replicating a similar preparation in school for those children that are not so fortunate poses immense problems for reception class teachers. They are faced with the demands of society that children should be taught to read as soon as possible and that all children should begin formally to learn to read sometime during the first year of schooling. But how can the work of an interested and involved parent, who is dealing with a child on a one to one basis, be crammed into a short period in school where the teacher has a whole class of children to deal with, all of whom are at various stages of readiness. (The term readiness is used here in terms of general awareness and understanding rather than as a set of specific skills.) Obviously, teachers facing such an intractable

Figure 1.1   *Reading begins early for the lucky ones!*

situation must be extremely well organised and highly sensitive to the needs of the children. A single general programme for all the children is not feasible and, without auxiliary help, adequate provision for those children who have been less well prepared by their home is virtually an impossibility.

During this period of preparation, and continuing when specific instruction begins, children must begin to understand that letters signify sounds, that groups of letters bounded by space signify words and that words have meaning. From this they will learn gradually that letters and words can be attached to what is said, thought or seen. In accomplishing this, and having learned the names of the letters of the alphabet for reference purposes, they will proceed to learn more specifically the sounds that can be attached to letters and to familiar common written words. The former they will learn in the context of words and the latter they will learn as wholes without undue analysis at this stage. (This does not mean that similarities of letters or sounds between words will not be pointed out in passing and that reference will not be made wherever possible to alliteration and words that rhyme. For as Adams (1992) has pointed out, although children have a working knowledge of phonemes as demonstrated by the fact that they can speak, it is not a conscious knowledge, whereas they are consciously aware of rhyme; therefore rhyme, and I would add alliteration are more 'attention grabbing'.)

In this process of looking at words and learning letter sounds, children will be learning that letters form spelling patterns that can be identified and transformed into the pronounceable sounds that make up words, whilst at the same time, concurrently, they will realise that words can be arranged in particular sequences so that they correspond to a meaningful statement.

This dual understanding of the significance of syllables in word recognition and of the composition of continuous prose is central to success in learning to read. The combination of the two is crucial on two accounts: it illuminates the nature of the task of breaking the code, and it ensures that this is done in such a way that the reader obtains a meaningful message whilst engaged upon the decoding task.

However, the period of preparation for learning to read cannot be regarded solely in terms of looking at books, words and letters and experiencing someone else reading books and labels. Everything we know about young children's learning suggests that they must be actively engaged in tasks from which they learn facts and how to deal with them and use them. Thus it is so important that exploratory or invented spelling and writing as well as oral story making should be an important aspect of prepa-ration for learning to read. In these activities children are beginning to learn how to construct words and compose texts. In many cases they are using bits of information that they have, such as knowing some letters with which they can represent words to varying degrees of approximation, and thus begin to compose their own texts. In searching for ways of expressing their thoughts on paper and, incidentally, trying to emulate adults, they will be engaged actively in beginning to understand both the code and the way in which texts are composed. If they know how a word is formed, then they will be in a position to recognise and identify it. Similarly, in order to comprehend a piece of prose they must be taught how to compose a text. Admittedly at first the texts will be very simple, but progress in reading, spelling and writing must proceed in unison, or roughly so. Hence it is unrealistic to consider teaching children to read in isolation from teaching them to spell and to write. Even the simplest form of writing, such as finger tracing letter-like shapes in a paint tray or the handwriting of single letters, contributes to their recognition. At a higher level, the composition of a text contributes to the effective under-standing of written English prose.

In many past discussions about reading, concern was mainly with facts that had to be learned. Little attention was paid to teaching children how to use those facts. Reading was regarded as being predominantly a process of recognition rather than as the utilisation of a variety of cues from which could be constructed meaningful thoughts. In order to understand fully what is involved in learning to read, so far as it affects what they do, children must be shown how to use the facts that they are learning. Unfortunately, this is not as simple as at first appears. The facts that can be learned, such as the sounds that can be attached to letters, letter strings, syllables and even some words, vary according to their setting. The letter *a* has at least two sounds, as have the other vowels, the digraph *ea* has at least nine sounds, the rime *ough* has several sounds as in *bough, cough* and *though*, and there are words such as *tears, row* and *read* which have two pronunciations and meanings, *bear* and *bare, meat* and *meet, seen* and *scene* which have different spellings and meanings but sound the same, as well as words such as *bear* and *saw* which have two meanings. The only way in which children can cope with this variety is to adopt a searching strategy in their approach to word recognition and in their interpretation of a text, and this they must be taught to do.

It is only natural that children, whilst grappling with the diffi-culty of applying the factual knowledge that they have of letter-sound correspondences, will endeavour to be satisfied with the first option that comes to mind. But this may be inadequate, and it is here, at this point, that context is a crucial factor. If the response is not appropriate to the context, the teacher should challenge the child to revise the response and to make one that is appropriate in the particular context. Occasionally, children will feel innately driven to search for an appropriate response where more than one is available, but they cannot be relied upon to react spontaneously in this self-correcting way unless they have been encouraged to develop a disposition for engaging in searching behaviour.

Therefore, in summary, it is the difficult task of teachers to inculcate three forms of behaviour in children who are learning to read.

1 Associative behaviour that enables children to match print with meaning and letters, letter strings, syllables and words with sounds. This involved memorising the symbols of print and their particular arrangement. Hence there must be a conscious effort on the part of children to memorise what amounts eventually to a full abstract symbolic code. The possibilities for confusion in these activities are great so it is the delicate task of teachers to couch memorisation within the context of language rather than to confine it entirely to the symbols themselves whilst ensuring that memorisation takes place.

2 Searching behaviour that enables children to use their knowledge of the variety in letter-sound correspondences and their increasing awareness of the spelling patterns and pronounceable syllables that form the basis of word recognition in reading, to search for appropriate responses to unfamiliar words. Both these forms of behaviour involve experimentation and flexibility on the part of the learners, and it is the teacher's task to show children how to experiment, how to try various alternatives, and how to arrive at a decision. Young children cannot be expected to adopt unaided these forms of behaviour in relation to print.

3 The third type of behaviour involves the formulation of ideas, information and story lines from the printed text. Again, young children cannot be expected to obtain clear messages from texts unless they are practised in this form of activity. If they become accustomed to reading aloud word by word, giving equal emphasis, tone and pace to each word, then it is not difficult to imagine their difficulties in recalling what has been read. This has been clearly demonstrated in recent research by Perera (1989) in Manchester. Children must be encouraged to search for meaningful strings of words within a given text, so that they proceed quickly to reading in phrases of variable length:

There / are / sweets / and / chocolates / in / the / sweet / shop
There are / sweets and chocolates / in the sweet shop
There are sweets and chocolates / in the sweet shop.

Children should also be expected to reflect upon what they read, even at the earliest stages, so that they become thoughtful appreciative readers and develop the habit of reviewing, even if momentarily, what has been read. To encourage this without making it burdensome is another of the delicate tasks of skilful teaching.

2 Some basic considerations

Given the complexity of learning to read and the inherent difficulties in teaching young children to read it is not surprising that there are some unresolved issues and several approaches to their resolution. Goswami and Bryant (1990) discuss the pros and cons of dividing readers into 'Phoenicians' and 'Chinese' as suggested by Baron and Treiman (1980) in the journal, *Memory and Cognition*, Vol. 8. Under this division it is argued that readers fall into one or other category: those who rely heavily upon a phonological approach through letter-sound correspondences to reading and named after the Phoenicians who invented the alphabetic system, and those who are largely dependent upon visual memory and named after the Chinese who have to remember word patterns. This is an interesting proposition and one which would be of great use especially in treating children who are finding learning to read unduly difficult. Unfortunately, as Goswami and Bryant conclude, the problem lies in identifying which child has which propensity. Problems such as this must wait further research, as must the problem of good readers who have difficulty in spelling some words, and several other unresolved issues.

However, teachers cannot wait for research to give them all the answers. They have to select methods and approaches that cover as many eventualities as possible. For example, they have to provide for both 'Phoenicians' and 'Chinese' approaches by using a mixture of techniques that include phonological approaches and exercise the visual memory.

Fortunately, teachers have much upon which to base their choice of methodology. There is the massive evaluation of research in the USA by Adams (1992), preceded by the work of E. J. Gibson, and in the United Kingdom there is the work of Bryant, Bradley, Goswami and Oakhill amongst others. There has been a extensive dissemination of ideas through the United Kingdom Reading Association and through in-service courses and conferences. It is on the basis of these various sources and extensive experience in classrooms that an attempt is made to draw out the essential aspects of technique in teaching children to read.

However, for students in training and for inexperienced teachers there is so much information, and indeed so much research that is inconclusive, that many find the subject matter rather confusing. It is the intention, therefore, in this section to identify some of the issues that arise when teachers are planning lessons on specific elements in reading. A number of questions are posed and a strong position is taken in response. This is not to imply that there is only one way of teaching and only one answer to each question. The position a teacher takes in answer to any of the questions depends upon several things. In the first place it is important that teachers are happy in what they are doing. Secondly, their experience and confidence will play a part, and, thirdly, much will depend upon the children they teach and the facilities that are available in terms of books, Information Technology (IT), and auxiliary help. So, the responses that are offered to the questions are meant to stimulate thought and perhaps to encourage young teachers to take up positions of their own from which they can proceed with confidence to formulate a programme of their own, which they can then compare with the programme that is outlined in Chapter 3.

Full programmes for the teaching of reading can only be formulated after due consideration of all the elements and issues that are encompassed within it. Even then, no matter how comprehensive its coverage, teachers will always feel the need to be free to make adjustments in the light of circumstances.

An overview of reading

What are the critical issues in learning to read?

Whilst attempting to cover adequately all that is suggested in the National Curriculum, in the National Literacy Strategy and in the proposals for a literacy hour, it is important that teachers ensure that children understand the basis of the various critical issues in a learning to read programme. These critical issues involve an understanding of the basis of each sub-skill of reading. For example, that texts convey meaning; that letters (graphemes) represent sounds (phonemes); that words are discrete entities; that there is an exact correspondence between the order of sounds spoken and the left to right sequence of words in a text, and that words arranged in a particular sequence corresponding to speech make sense; that words are composed of letters and clusters of letters to which sounds can be attached in such a way as to produce a meaningful word, as opposed to a nonsense word or a nonsensical sound, sl-ight-ly as opposed to s-l-i-g-h-t-l-y; that there is a pattern in spelling which has a regularity which can be relied upon, except in certain cases which, nevertheless, form sub-groups of correspondingly constructed words; that the words in a text are so arranged that anticipation can to a great extent be relied upon when reading; that attention to phrases leads to rhythmic reading (rather than word by word reading) with variations in emphasis helping to elucidate the meaning of the text; that a conscious effort must be made at all stages of reading a text to retain at least the essence of the textual message, and that where details are an important element in the text then an extra effort must be made to retain the information; and, finally, that reflection upon what has been read is an essential habit that must be acquired if reading is to add to the reader's mental store of experiences and knowledge.

It is understanding the essence of these sub-skills and having been taught to use them to draw analogies in an experimental and searching way that will enable children to cope with the perplexities and myriad details that comprise the skill of reading. Although children will have to be continually learning new details, in order to avoid being overwhelmed they will have to be shown how to relate details to generalisations of what is possible with those details. This is the type of platform that children must be given to enable them to build a more detailed knowledge of each sub-skill, whilst at the same time relating it to other sub-skills. In other words, they must acquire a facility in the use of rules and conventions which they can then apply in new circumstances and, whilst in the process of doing this, they must experience the relationship between the word level (phonographemic cues), the sentence level (syntactic or grammatical cues) and the text level (semantic cues).

Teaching the alphabet

When should we teach children the names of the letters of the alphabet?

All the indications from research are that those children who learn the alphabet off by heart, and frequently as a chant to the tune of 'Twinkle twinkle little star', before attending school eventually become good readers. This may indicate a supportive parental interest that is cumulative over the whole period when children are learning to read. Additionally, however, a case can be made that it is advantageous for children to learn the names of letters of the alphabet uncluttered and unconfused by subsequent learning of the sound-letter correspondences and their impact within words, which is a far more complex thing to learn. It is easy for children with their known propensity for learning rhymes and jingles to learn what is in effect another chant: AB CD E,F,G; HI JK LMNOP; (Twinkle, twinkle . . .). Accompanying such a chant children will enjoy looking at one of the many superb alphabet ABC books that are available, identifying the pictures orally and associating the printed letters with the spoken word. Some people use the device of saying: 'A (the name of the letter) is for apple' with emphasis on the /æ/[1] sound in the word thus associating the name and the sound of the letter. In this way the child acquires a useful point of reference that will make him feel familiar with print; it is very difficult to deal with something that does not have a clear and precise identifiable label. It will have been also an easy way of conveying to the young child the notion that print can be attached to sounds made by the child, and thus it has the effect of launching the naive young child upon an understandable and logical approach to learning to read. Finally, the child will have acquired at an appropriate age, and in a suitable manner, the basic knowledge upon which can be built later an understanding of alphabetical order, necessary for referencing in the later stages of learning to use one's reading skills.

There are, however, several other reasons for ensuring that children become familiar with the alphabet. Durrell (1968), addressing the 12th Annual Convention of the International Reading Association in the USA, pointed out that the names of all the letters of the alphabet, except the vowels and *h, q, w* and *y,* contain their phonemes plus an extraneous vowel. In the case of *b, c, d, g, p, t* and *v,* the phoneme is followed by the name of the vowel *e: /bi:/, /ci:/, /di:/, /gi:/, /pi:/, /ti:/, /vi:/.* In the case of *f, l, m, n, s* and *x,* the phoneme is preceded by the vowel *e* in its phonemic form: */ef/, /el/, /em/, /en/, /es/, /ex/.* The letters *r, j, k* and *y* similarly contain their phomemes, but in their case the vowel phonemes /æ/, /ei/ and /ai/ are involved: *r* = /æ r/, *j* and *k* = /jei/ and /kei/ respectively and *y* = /waij/. And if this idea of a phonemic presence in the names of letters is carried a little further, even *h* and *q* have something of their sounds in their names: /eitʃ/ and /ku:/, the former at the end of the sound combination and the latter at the beginning; whilst /z/ and /w/ are clearly discernible in their names: /z/ at the beginning and /w/ at the end.

Durrell pointed out that this close association between the phonemes and the names of letters contributed to subsequent success in learning the sounds that can be attached to letters. Hence, familiarity with the names of the letters of the alphabet

---

[1] The symbols indicating pronunciation are those of the International Phonetic Alphabet listed at the end of the book. Their use avoids ambiguity.

should have a prominent place in preparing children for their introduction to learning to read. If children acquire English spelling patterns visually by osmosis as suggested by the work of Gibson and Levin (1975), it is reasonable to assume that they will acquire the beginnings of a phonic knowledge of written English similarly by osmosis. Thus, imperceptibly, children who know the names of the letters of the alphabet will imbibe and assimilate the sounds that can be attached to letters.

Other reasons for learning the alphabet are the probabilities that in the process of becoming familiar with the names of the letters of the alphabet, children will learn to discriminate between symbolic shapes, acquire a disposition for making fine distinctions between letter-shapes, such as between *B* and *D*, *b* and *p*, *M*, *W* and *N*, *c* and *o*, *o* and *a*, and eventually, with further experiences of print in various forms, come gradually to understand the symbolic nature of print.

When children enter primary schools without being able to recite the alphabet, it seems a very easy task to teach it at the outset before the complexities of the sound-spelling system have to be tackled. Naturally some children will prove more adept than others, as in all aspects and at all stages of learning.

The danger is, of course, that over-enthusiastic parents may attempt to force the issue and treat any slowness of response as a sign of impending failure. The suggestion here is that knowledge of the alphabet should be gathered gradually and incidentally to the enjoyment of looking at ABC books, discussing the pictures and pretending to 'read' the letters. Any chanting of the alphabet would only follow these engaging activities with the books.

Preparation for learning to read

How can parents prepare children for learning to read?
It is essential for children to know that print conveys a message but it is very difficult to explain this to them whilst they are so young. Therefore it must be demonstrated in a way that captures their attention.

This can be done both in the home and in the school in several ways. Most importantly, it can be done by reading aloud stories that they want to hear and, in the process, pointing out to them in passing significant words such as titles, names of characters, animals and objects. Children can also come to realise that labels on tins, jars and boxes in the kitchen and on features in the school indicate what is in those receptacles and the purpose of the features. They can also have pointed out to them notices on buses, in the street, and on the road – Chester, Candy Shop, Stop – and they can eventually search for their initials in street and house names.

In this process, spread over a long period of time, some children will learn to recognise certain familiar words, such as, corn flakes, stop, bus stop, sugar, tea, biscuit, sweets and the names of members of the family.

Some parents will encourage the children to 'pretend to write', and seize upon any opportunity to write the child's message out, so that, fleetingly, the child may draw comparisons between what that child has 'written' and what the parent has written. This presupposes that the child will have had lots of opportunities for finger painting and the use of paint brushes in order to develop muscular movement of the fingers and hands.

Finally, children will be encouraged to participate in 'reading' along with the parent well-known rhymes and nursery rhymes as well as joining in the known repetitious parts of folk tales. Tape cassettes and IT software can be used for this purpose, but they cannot replace the personal touch of the parent or teacher.

Starting with whole words

Should we introduce whole words first, before starting on phonics?

To introduce whole words first has been a feature of much teaching and was an essential ingredient of what was known as the 'Look and Say' method, the main exponents of which were F. J. Schonell in the United Kingdom and A. I. Gates in the USA.

Recognition of whole words can be simplistic and uncomplicated by specific analysis, relying to a great extent upon memory and thereby it is not very confusing to a child who has little experience of the elements within words. Children are presented with words, told what they represent and then they memorise them through meeting them repeatedly.

By using whole words emphasis can be on meaning, that is contextual meaning, that is concrete and something a child is aware of, rather than on sound-spelling correspondences which are abstract in nature.

This means that words can be seen in the context of their meaning by children, thus illustrating that printed words can be associated with the child's thoughts and what he wants to say, which is a logical approach to print as a second signalling system. Children have a primary or first signalling system in their spoken language; now they are about to learn an extension of that system, hence the logic of attaching print to speech in the first place, rather than the other way round of attaching sounds to print.

The words arising from children's thoughts and experiences can be strung together to form a text which conforms relatively closely to those thoughts and statements of experiences. For example, *water, bowl, sand, tray* can be readily transformed by a teacher, in the sight of the children, into, *We are playing with water in the bowl and sand in the tray*.

However, there is another motive for introducing children to a fair number of common words before beginning a closer phonic analysis of words. If these words are used by teachers and children in the sense that a child is expected to pick out the jar containing 'red paint' or to label the window with the appropriate word, and if the children have to select from an albeit limited number of such labels, they will be developing strategies for comparing, contrasting and distinguishing words. In these circumstances, with continuing practice and experience, children will be picking up knowledge about individual letters and groups of letters in an incidental but highly effective way. After all, if children have to identify the paint they require by its label before they may use it, then the impetus to look carefully at the labels and make comparisons is strong. These activities form a bridge between recognition of a few very common words and the phonic analysis that will be necessary in order to recognise unfamiliar but widely used words that will appear in the early reading books.

Phonics

Why introduce phonics?

It would be laborious and wasteful of time and of the advantages offered by an alphabetic system to learn every word needed for reading as a discrete and idiosyncratic construction. For the majority of people it would be an impossible task. The alphabet offers a severely constrained number of items, letters of the alphabet and letter strings and their corresponding sounds, to be learned rather than having to learn thousands of word characters that cannot be analysed. It must be remembered that many thousands of words are constructed from twenty-six letters. All we need to know are the various sounds that can be attached to these letters and the sounds of a limited number of combinations of some letters. We must then develop a disposition to generalise and to search for a meaningful sound representation of the word under scrutiny by flexibly applying the various possible sound-outcomes until a response is achieved that fits the context. For instance, if beginners are familiar with the words *chick* and *chicken* and have some knowledge of letter sounds and are confronted with the unfamiliar word *chocolate*, they have a good chance of starting with the appropriate first sound /tʃ/ for *ch*. If, in addition, emphasis had been given in the early stages to the alternative vowel sounds rather than only to the vowel sounds which correspond to the vowel name and which occur as interrupted digraphs (cake, coke), then the next four letters of the word are relatively easy /tʃ/, /ɔ/, /k/, /ɔ/, /l/. Even if the reader then continues with the simple vowel sound /æ/ for *a* as in *cat* the emerging meaning would, or should, act as a corrective, provided the child has been encouraged to search for meaning as well as for sound.

The above example illustrates clearly why contextual meaning should enter into phonic interpretation wherever possible. Phonics are essential, but they can easily become abstract and confusing if isolated from a simultaneous search for meaning.

Phonemic awareness in children should not be taken for granted. It is a necessary element in learning to read, and it must first be fostered and specifically demonstrated by teachers, with instruction continuing until a sufficiently advanced ability in word recognition has been achieved for teachers to rely upon children to formulate word-attack strategies unaided. Meanwhile teachers have to take every opportunity to 'sound out' words, to draw comparisons with words of a similar structure and to encourage children to do likewise.

Difficulties in teaching phonics

What difficulties have to be overcome in teaching phonics?

Phonemes, commonly referred to as letter sounds, are pure and cannot stand alone. They are the sounds as heard when a word is pronounced normally and as a complete uninterrupted entity. The sounds of the letters if pronounced separately degenerate into /bə:/, /a:r/, and /tə:/, (ber, ar, ter) for example, which is not a close representation of the normal sound attached to *bat*. Nevertheless, these distortions, if not taken to extremes, can be quite close to the pure forms of the phonemes; close enough that is, to act as a firm indicator of the required sound. It simply requires teaching that expects searching and flexible behaviour on the part of the learner, and it is up to the teacher to demonstrate this flexibility and searching activity.

Thus, as required in the above reference to the word *chocolate*, having given the inappropriate sound response to the letter *a* so that the resulting pronunciation was /tʃ/, ɔ, k, ɔ, *l* æ, t/, the reader, if processing the emerging sound in a search for a meaningful response and realising that something is wrong, will try an alternative pronunciation using the /ei/ sound for the letter *a*, or even

/ut/ and thereby get closer to the actual sound of the word he knows.

Obviously, the fact that there are alternative sounds that can be attached to such letters as the vowels, the diphthongs and the consonants *c* and *g*, does pose problems for the beginner. However, there seems to be little point in evading the issue by postponing confrontation with the alternatives. For instance, the words *am*, *have* and *cake* are going to appear in the early reading materials, so it is advisable to make a virtue out of necessity and teach children the alternative sounds. In fact a strong argument can be made for suggesting that learning is made easier when the learner is offered the opportunity to compare two or three alternatives. It creates a yardstick for learning a particular item and its variants and, in the case of alternative letter sounds, it creates a disposition for diversity, as Harlow put it, so that children do not over-rely upon regularity and adapt the dual approach of searching for sound and meaning. In this approach meaning then acts as a corrective and illustrates the importance of dealing with phonics in the context of words in their setting.

Where diphthongs are concerned, the alternatives in some cases are many. Consider the diphthong *ea* in *bear, bean, beautiful, idea, ocean, heard, break, cereal*. These are for the most part common words, so the issue of their identification cannot be avoided for long. While to introduce them all simultaneously would seem silly, it would seem sensible to deal with each version as it occurred, ensuring that a serious attempt is made to learn the word in question. As words with alternative sounds of *ea* occur, the learner can associate them with the previously encountered versions. In this way children would learn each version in its natural setting and, after the first encounter, begin to build up a knowledge of all the versions.

It would be unrealistic to expect beginners to remember all of them, but at least they will be gaining some idea of the alternatives whilst at the same time learning to exercise a disposition to try a range of possibilities aided by the semantic cues provided in the context. Effective teachers make learning situations memorable for children. They do not simply refer to the subject matter; they try to enhance its interest for the learners. For example, when encountering the word *bear*, a humorous aside could be made by the teacher to the effect that this word refers to an animal with brown or black fur and which walks on four legs and not to the naughty little bare boy running naked down the street.

Another strategy in helping beginners to identify words is to help them to look for boundaries within words other than those delineated by individual letters. A first step is to look for two-letter blends:

bl . . . , br . . . , dr . . . , cl . . . , ch . . . , cr . . . , tr . . . , gr . . . ,
and so on,
. . . ld, . . . rd, . . . rt, . . . ng, and so on,
shr . . . , str . . . , and so on.

It is futile to allow beginners to struggle with these blends by pronouncing each letter separately followed by a stumbling attempt to blend them. It is far better to teach these blends as a single unit rather than as three or four steps. Word families can be compiled to illustrate the sounds:

tram, train, trick, track
cold, hold, fold.

This should be done not as a stiff academic exercise but as a game of 'Think of a word that begins like . . .'. Subsequently, letter strings which can cause difficulty because of the complexity of the phonemic combinations within them, should be taught as one unit:

tion as /ʃən/ in *station, caution, competition,*
able as /ei, b, ə, l,/ in *table,* and subsequently as /ə, b, ə, l/ in *comfortable,*
ious as /ʃəz/ in *furious, precious,*
ight as /ait/ rather than persist with an /i/, /g/, /h/, /t/ split.

These can be dealt with separately as they appear in the reading scheme or books. Great success has been achieved by teachers pointing out the larger pronounceable units within words such as, in referring to the word *examination*, they have pronounced it for the child as, /eks - æm/, /in/, /eiʃən/, and they have indicated that the word *clearly* has three parts, /kl/, /iəɾ/, /li/, and not seven as indicated by the letters. This activity by teachers, in directing attention by example to the ways in which it is possible to process a word in manageable units, is the essence for effective teaching of word attack skills. The work of Fernald (1943) in Los Angeles earlier this century bears witness to the efficacy of this procedure.

Recent research by Bryant, Bradley and Goswami in England and the report by Adams in America have shown that children's sense of rhyme and rhythm can help with both word recognition and with the comprehension of texts. In order to take advantage of this, many teachers when introducing word attack skills have presented words in the form of *b - at, c - at, pr - am, tr - am, l - ight, f - ight.* This form has the advantage of catching the rhyming instinct of the children and, additionally, it has enabled teachers to draw up word families with the words in each family ending with the same rime but having different onsets. For example, *sick, stick, prick, kick, lick* and *Mick*. Through such word families, children will be practised in drawing comparisons between words and in using the model to make comparisons in other words. They will be provided also with a manageable way of splitting syllables, an advantage when they come face to face with polysyllabic words of greater complexity such as, *formulate, nourishment, refrigerator*, and so on.

This division of syllables into onset and rime (*br* is the onset and *ead* is the rime in the word *bread*) makes it easy for children to detect corresponding rimes and should be utilised as such. It makes comparisons easier, and it facilitates word analysis. However, there is another side to word recognition that involves blending the component, that is, pronounceable, parts of words. Word identification involves both analysis and synthesis. Hence, although *br - ead* enables young learners to call up prior knowledge of words like *h - ead* and *d - ead* for instance, the split between onset and rime does cause a jerkiness in pronunciation, whereas *brea - d*, like *hea - d* and *dea - d* blends more smoothly and is truer to a normal pronunciation of the word as a complete unit. Therefore, the conclusion must be that children must be trained to use both ways of splitting words: one way to help in the identification process, and the other to facilitate the pronunciation process.

Looking for letter sounds and clusters and identifying the parts of words – syllables, onsets and rimes – should not be regarded as exercises in the old sense of set lessons. It will be more effective if it is encouraged incidentally for very short but frequently recurring periods during the varied activities of a normal progressive infant school.

The importance of meaning

What part does meaning play in learning to read?

As suggested above, provided children are taught to employ flexible strategies in word identification, meaning will enter to resolve any uncertainty. In trying to identify the word *chocolate*, a child might try /tʃ, ɔ, k, ɔ, l, æ, t/ and reject it because it does not sound as English as could be expected. At a revised attempt /tʃ, ɔ, k, ɔ, l, ei, t/, rhyming with *late* may emerge, but meaning and familiarity of pronunciation will probably connect this with the more usual /tʃ, ɔ, k, ɔ, l, u, t/ – a quite normal pronunciation of the word *chocolate* rhyming with *bullet*.

Some emphasis on the extraction of meaning also helps where

children are struggling with a sentence or prose passage and manage successfully to identify a reasonable proportion of the words, but have to guess unfamiliar and unusual words, or words whose spelling patterns are complex.

Furthermore, as the children progress they can speed up their reading by anticipating, very loosely, what is coming. To enable this to happen, again it is up to the teacher to create a disposition for thinking about what is being read. Two very effective measures spring to mind. First there are short sessions with a small group reading from an overhead projector familiar nursery rhymes which have the ends of lines or some complete lines omitted. The group reads in unison what is shown and individuals are called upon to fill in the gaps orally. Secondly, there is the practice of asking children to recall what they have read, whether it be a sentence, a paragraph or a complete story. These are just two ways of inculcating a disposition to consciously think as one reads.

Even as adults we find unexpected texts difficult, in that our reading rate is reduced, making comprehension even more difficult. Thus it can be argued that, in the case of their early reading books, children should know the contents of those books before they begin to read them. For this reason, and others, nursery rhymes and folk tales have been suggested as suitable for early reading. The children know, or should know, many of the more common nursery rhymes and folk tales; and in any case they are easily learned. (The reason that they have lasted down the ages is that they are so memorable.) In trying to read texts that they already know orally, the young learners will be able to concentrate more effectively upon the words of the text, for they will have in mind a knowledge of the meaning of the text to help them in their identification of the words.

One course of difficulty during the early stages of learning to read is a tendency to concentrate or centre solely upon one element of reading such as a response to a letter or groups of letters within a word without reference to meaning. This is frequently the cause of a child 'getting stuck on a word'. The teacher's task is then to encourage the child to search for a possible meaning from the context in which the problem word is encountered. Young children need to become practised in the combined use of phonic skills and semantic cues.

The place of guessing

What part should guessing play in reading a text where some words are unfamiliar?

If guessing is not considered totally random, but rather as the consideration of plausible hypotheses, as Kagan, an American psychologist, considered it to be, then it has an important part to play in helping children to decode and interpret a text. In this guise guessing can be regarded as an aspect of searching behaviour whereby children can hold in mind the meanings they have gathered and use them to help in decoding the problem word.

However, children must not be allowed to think that prediction is all that is necessary in interpreting an unfamiliar word or phrase. Attention must be applied simultaneously to the actual print and any cues picked up from the problem word should be considered in combination with the predicted meaning as a form of cross-referencing.

Hence, practice in prediction is a useful training in reflection upon texts which Lunzer and Gardner (1979) in *The Effective Use of Reading* regarded as that which distinguishes good from weak readers, but it is also a useful aid to the more usual word identification skills.

Real books or reading schemes

Real books or reading schemes, which?

The counter-question is, why not both? The real books approach originated during the late 1970s and early 1980s because some people believed that the published reading schemes were poorly written in terms of literary quality and, in spite of misleading advertisements, were hardly scientifically constructed. These people felt it was important that children should encounter, from the beginning, good literature and that any grading of the degree of difficulty of these books could be controlled through the teacher's choice of books. They were influenced by Frank Smith's statement that one can only learn to read by reading, which is true in the way in which he meant it. Unfortunately, some people have oversimplified his intentions and have virtually ignored what Smith has to say on learning to distinguish between the various features of letters and words. However, any interpretation that helps to enrich a classroom with good literature should be welcomed enthusiastically.

Liz Waterland and Margaret Meek were instrumental in advocating what has become known as an apprentice approach to reading, in which the teacher talked to children about a particular book, read it aloud to the children while they followed the text and were encouraged to join in. In this way it was thought that the children would witness and eventually understand how reading was done. In order to get the flavour of this approach students should read *How Texts Teach What Readers Learn* by M. Meek and *Read with Me: An Apprenticeship Approach to Reading* by L. Waterland.

In the argument, real books or reading schemes, can be seen emerging two separate issues: one concerning the quality of the texts, the other concerning the methodology of teaching children to read. No argument can be raised against the choice of good literature; the only consideration is whether teachers have the time to select a range of good children's literature, and then to classify it in terms of the difficulty of the text and of its provision of adequate practice of all the aspects of decoding and textual interpretation. Even using 'real' books and an apprenticeship arrangement of instruction, it must surely be argued that teachers still have to plan in advance for seemingly spontaneous reactions to developments in the child's reading progress. They still need a programme of instruction and practice in order that children may learn the code, otherwise instruction will be haphazard and will lack the depth and rigour that most children require.

It is at this point in the argument that many teachers settle for a published reading scheme. Throughout the 1980s, we saw a vast improvement in literary quality and built-in instructional development in reading schemes. Many teachers think that they provide a good basis for instruction which can be supplemented in two ways: one, by introducing 'real' books alongside the scheme, and the other by adding their own programme of instruction to that embodied in the texts of the reading scheme. Suggestions are offered for such a programme of instruction in Chapter 3. It could be implemented alongside the use of a 'real books' approach, or it may be used to supplement work suggested by a teachers' manual accompanying a published reading scheme.

One reading scheme, published by Macmillan and edited by Dr Joyce Morris, called *Language in Action*, is based on a clear programme of phonic development – a programme which Morris calls Phonics 44, to which reference is made in Chapter 6. The books within the scheme are written by accredited children's authors, so the development of language patterns is not stilted. This scheme, to which further improvements are about to be made, could be used alongside the programme proposed in Chapter 3. It would provide a detailed practice basis for the various word attack skills, that are referred to in the programme that I suggest, covering all the elements in English words.

Needless to say, other reading schemes such as Ginn's *Reading 360*, Arnold-Wheaton's *Story Chest* and Oxford's *Reading Tree* which may not have the overt commitment to a clearly defined phonic programme that is the central feature of *Language in Action*, could be readily used alongside the programme that is proposed in Chapter 3. All of these modern schemes have their strengths, and their choice is to a large extent a matter of teacher preference. No matter which reading scheme is used, the teaching programme will have to be adjusted to fit in with it, in order to meet the varying needs of children and to suit the teaching style of individual teachers.

If to this combination of published reading scheme and programme for the development of reading is added an array of 'real books' by established children's authors at every reading level, the result will be a comprehensive approach to teaching children to read: one that embodies a strong motivational basis, an integrated and interrelated teaching programme covering reading, spelling and writing, and a reading scheme that ensures at least a minimum coverage of all aspects of word identification, a full range of language patterns and variety in textual arrangements. It is only by employing such a comprehensive approach that children of all abilities and dispositions towards reading will be taught adequately.

For those teachers who are in a position to select a reading scheme and choose individual books to supplement that scheme, Perera's research, reported in Beard (1993), provides invaluable guidance. She examined a selection of books from five recent reading schemes, *New Way, Reading 360, Reading Tree, Story Chest* and *Book Bus*, and a carefully selected group, nine in all, of individual or 'real' books. In doing so she established a number of useful pointers for choosing not only between these schemes and books but also for making a selection amongst any future publications and for deciding upon the ratio of reading scheme to individual books. The criteria suggested are:

- the stories must be well-formed in the sense that each should flow naturally to a satisfying conclusion;
- the prose should be rhythmical and the sentence patterns should not sound alien to the child;
- short sentences will tend to help struggling readers, although some variation in length will bring variety to the text (and, I would add, will help to promote further familiarity with a range of language patterns);
- the appropriate use of pronouns avoiding laborious repetition of nouns, and the use of familiar reduced forms such as *I've* and *don't*, etc., help to make the child feel at ease with the text;

- repetition of words to aid learning whilst necessary should not assume a stilted or contrived form, and where the repetition of words is inadequate, as in the case of individual or real books as well as some parts of reading schemes, then the teacher must be prepared to make additional provision for the child to re-encounter new words.

In addition to Perera's chapter, teachers at all stages in the primary school will find Tucker's chapter on the literary and developmental aspects, and Littlefair's discussion of the non-narrative aspects of 'good books' extremely helpful and enlightening (Beard, 1993).

Shared and paired reading

What about shared reading and paired reading?

None of what was written under the section *Real books or reading schemes* above is meant to suggest that shared or paired reading have no place. They have a very important place. Shared reading occurs when a teacher takes a child through a reading book, not as one who checks the reader, but as the initiator and, in the first place, main reader, with the child following the text and joining in where possible. This is an admirable thing to do with hesitant readers, using known texts such as nursery rhymes and folk tales or stories made up by the child and transcribed by the teacher. Stories with repetitive passages are particularly good for building up confidence in the reader (Figure 2.1).

This shared activity creates a warm participatory enjoyment of a literary pursuit. It provides opportunities for teachers to react to stories as they proceed and to comment upon various aspects of the text: new words and phrases, apt descriptions, the events in the story and, periodically, to draw comparisons between words and events in the story with those in previously read stories. Meek's book, referred to earlier, is a good launching pad for the hesitant young teacher.

As ability in reading increases, children will take over the initiative in reading with teachers playing a prompting or supportive role. Some of this prompting can be designed to guide children into more expressive reading, so that they were weaned away from word by word reading into reading in phrases and sentences, so that meaning emerges more noticeably as the reading proceeds.

Paired reading, whereby two children read together, can be used for a similar purpose. Frequently, junior school children are taught how to write stories for young children, and they are then

Figure 2.1 *'Let's each read it and see who can make it sound easy to understand.'*

allowed to try the stories out with children in infant classes. Instructionally, they are not able to emulate fully the role of the teacher, but they can bring freshness to the reading lesson!

Children of equal ability can use paired reading to share what they have written or to practise reading. It is a good device to occupy children gainfully and to teach them to co-operate and help others. It is surprising how much help and support children can give each other (Figure 2.2).

Writing and reading combined

Should the teaching of reading be combined with the teaching of writing?

The answer is, yes! And the reason is fairly obvious. Learning to write gives the child another perspective on print. It is seen from the constructional side as well as from the decoding and comprehension side. Handwriting introduces the construction and form of letters to children in a more concentrated way than allowing children merely to look at them; it emphasises the constituent elements within words; and it gives children a feel for words in

Figure 2.2　*Children helping and supporting one another.*

a kinaesthetic sense. When adults are asked to spell an unusual word, frequently they will write it out tentatively, which suggests a kinaesthetic element in their learning and memory. Furthermore, having to write and spell a word concentrates the mind and helps to reactivate visual memory traces of spelling patterns, to explore sound-letter correspondences and to impress images upon the memory.

One aspect of this is of particular importance during the early stages of learning to read and that is what may be called exploratory writing and invented spelling, whereby young children pretend that they are writing a story or a word, and, in doing so, they try to write and to spell the words that they require. In order to do this they use what limited knowledge they have of sound-letter relationships and of letter formation, usually on a single letter and phoneme basis, and eventually somewhat later in their development they consciously try to reactivate visual memory traces of spelling patterns that have impinged upon their minds from their experiences in an environment with print everywhere, albeit very hazily in the early stages. Read (1971), writing in the *Harvard Educational Review*, Vol. 41, found that pre-school children who have not yet learned to read can get very near to spelling words that they need for their stories, such as DA (day) LADE (lady) ALRVATA (elevator) ACHRAY (ashtray), showing in some instances visual memory of spelling patterns and in others the application of an emerging knowledge of sound-letter corre-spondences. Goswami and Bryant (1990), referring to Read's work, show that there can be a meticulous attention to the sounds as they know them at the time by children in these early stages, and they give as an example the production of CR to represent car where the child knows how to represent the sound /k/ but mistakenly represents the rime *ar* with the letter R. The same confusion can be seen in DA and LADE above. This misuse of incomplete knowledge and its resultant intermingling of letter sounds and letter names is akin to what Peter Herriot called virtuous errors when referring to the use of 'the sheeps' and 'I finded' as indicating a knowledge of one aspect of the rule of plurals and one for the rule for constructing the past tense.

Although Goswami and Bryant distinguish between the early stages of reading where onset and rime predominate in the child's approach and the early explorations in spelling where the emphasis is on the use of phonemes, that is, a letter by letter approach, nevertheless there is ample research to show that five- and six-year-old children are rapidly acquiring incidentally, without specific teaching, the fundamental spelling patterns of English. They find it easier to remember such nonsense syllables as *mur* than to remember trigrams like *mru* which do not form English spelling patterns (Gibson and Levin, 1975). As this result emerged with children who were totally deaf, so the ease of pronouncing the former syllables did not come into it. The conclusion that must be drawn from this evidence that children find themselves compelled to explore the spelling system, is that teachers should encourage it, give greater prominence to it than simply remarking upon the effort, and use it as a basis for devel-oping the children's understanding of the spelling system. Without discouraging the younger children, the teacher and the child can 'compare notes', with the teacher showing how he or she would write what the child has written. In doing so, further impressions are made upon the mind of the child. Hence, the child is contin-ually revising patterns of spelling by his own efforts and through those of the teacher.

It is not only spelling and word recognition that benefit from combining reading and writing. Just as reading to children helps them to develop further their language patterns, so composing their own stories helps to activate and consolidate the language patterns that they have acquired. It is the composition and compiling of texts that illuminates language written by others and helps in the comprehension of texts written by others.

Spelling

What should be done about spelling?

The first thing is to acknowledge that it is important. Society judges people by their spelling, albeit irrationally. Gone are the days when some teachers thought that emphasis on spelling could be postponed until children learned to express themselves. They believed that emphasis on spelling would inhibit thought about the message to be conveyed, as indeed an over-emphasis on spelling would. Nowadays it is widely thought that spelling needs some carefully designed attention. However, it would be unwise to over-stress it and make it an inhibiting factor because children could become neurotic about it, but emphasis can be tempered with reasonableness.

Spelling ability emerges with experience of words. It is not something that can be taught in a few sessions. First, children learn to spell specific words through exploratory spelling activity depending heavily upon letter-sound relationships, and gradually they begin to imbibe the spelling patterns and, eventually, the conventions, as was indicated in the previous section. They do this according to Goswami and Bryant by drawing analogies with what words they know, applying awareness of rime and making inferences.

However, children need to be given guidance to supplement the learning by osmosis that is taking place naturally, and to have their attention drawn over a long period of time to the elements in words: single letters, letter strings, syllables and their corresponding sounds and the spelling patterns of English, so that they are moved on imperceptibly from their original over-reliance on phonemes. The more a word is seen, and the more frequently it is seen, the greater the chance that the child will learn to spell it. But it must not be forgotten that seeing is not enough for many children. There is such a thing as the passive gaper – one who looks without really registering what is seen, and we can all lapse into that! Therefore in teaching a child to spell there are three essentials.

1 The child must be shown how the word is pronounced such as /pen-sil/ for *pencil*, or /br/, /ed/ and /bre/, /d/ for *bread*, and attention must be drawn to the printed sections of the word as that word is pronounced. Word cards can be bent to demonstrate the boundaries for sounding words such as:

| fl | ow | ers | | str | ing | and | stri | ng | .

This approach coincides with showing a child how to read a word.

2 The child must participate actively in spelling the word. The best way is for the teacher to split the word orally, as above, and get the child to try to spell it (exploratory spelling). The teacher can make any necessary corrections to the child's attempt, and this should be followed by the conscious learning of the word. A well-tried way of doing this is for the child to trace with the forefinger the word saying the constituent parts as illustrated by the teacher, and then to try to write the word without copying. If the child fails, the process should be repeated until success is achieved; and when it is, the teacher should make a great fuss of that success.

3 This learning must be reinforced whenever possible by repeating the process outlined under 2 above, within the hour, at the end of the day, the following day, the following week and at half-term, otherwise it will simply be forgotten.

As children progress in their response to the spelling system and acquire the conventions, they must be made aware that spelling contains several eccentricities: the interrupted digraph as in *cake* and *gate*, which can subsequently be shown to apply in the case of each vowel, so that, eventually, children are able to generalise the rule of a long vowel, if followed by a consonant plus the letter *e*; the silent letters as in *gnaw, light*; the mismatch between some spellings and the corresponding sounds as in *mission*, where *ss* becomes /ʃ/ in sound; and the fact that prefixes and suffixes can affect the meaning of words, as in *out-run* and *unnecessary*, eventually being able to distinguish between the meanings of *uninterested* and *disinterested* and other such fine distinctions. Notice of these cases, the search for them and the use of them can become a detective operation, a language search to achieve a particular end, and as such can intrigue children. The same detective work can be applied to the spelling of place names of Anglo-Saxon or Viking derivation and to surnames denoting occupations.

There comes time when children need to realise that sound is not the only key to spelling. In addition to looking for phonological associations, children must be trained to look for and remember graphemic patterns which defy logical association with the normal conventions of sound-spelling relationships. Visual memory is crucial when confronted with the task of spelling *said* and *afraid, come* and *home, laugh* and *caught, took* and *poor*, and the variations in sound caused by the digraph *ea* in such words as *idea, measure, team, ocean, beautiful, bear, great, create, meander*. Also, having learned the normal convention of the interrupted digraph in words like *home* and *mite*, the words *come* and *might* have to be committed to visual memory.

Cripps and Peters (1990) stress the importance of visual learning in connection with spelling, emphasising that phonics as part of spelling activity is only part of the answer. Much will also depend on visual memory as in the case of *across* with one *c* and *account, access* and *accident* with two *c*s, and *occasion* with one *s* and *mission* with double *s*.

Does writing prose enhance comprehension?

How can learning to write continuous prose help children who are learning to read?

Just as it was suggested that learning to spell and to write words correctly helped to illuminate the constituent parts of words, so it is that composing and writing a text introduces children to the ways in which meaning is conveyed and thereby contributes to their abilities to comprehend what is written.

First, children learn that what they want to say can be written down. For instance, they draw a picture, and the teacher asks what it is they want written down. At the same stage of development, they are trying to write for themselves. The teacher transcribes their attempts and reads the outcome together with them. Subsequently, they learn to write imaginative stories and accurate descriptions of actions and events, and increasingly to conform to the conventions of written as opposed to spoken language. Finally, they learn to write for an audience, adjusting what is written to meet the exigencies of the situation and the needs of the audience. At every stage, children must be encouraged to read and reread what they have written, and then ask themselves whether it is an exact portrayal of what was intended to be said. Naturally, at first it will be the teacher who asks the question for them, but from the teacher's questions children will learn to question themselves and, thereby, to examine their own texts and subsequently, other texts critically.

A further advantage to be gained from getting the children to write and then to read their own texts is that it is much easier to get them to put expression into their rereading, if done aloud, because they know how they want to say it. From this it then becomes easy to encourage them to read with variable stress, tone and pace and to regard texts as meaningful chunks of words rather than a conglomeration of single words.

Reading helps writing

How can reading enhance the ability to write and, in particular, to compose a text?

When children are reading published material, various attributes in the text should be pointed out to them. For example, the captivating openings of some of the Beatrix Potter tales, the intriguing opening to *The Iron Man* by Ted Hughes and the wonderful ending to *Mrs Frisby and the Rats of Nimh* can be discussed and appreciated. Similarly, there can be comment upon descriptions and imagery in poetry, all of which helps to sensitise children to the use of language.

Naturally the level of comment and discussion will vary according to the age of the children. What is important is that references should be made to beginnings, endings and particular aspects of stories to illuminate structure and effect. With infants, after a captivating or intriguing opening to a story, a simple comment such as, 'what is going to happen?', interjected before proceeding with the story, will suffice. With older juniors a more critical discussion may take place after reading the complete story. The essence of these activities is to direct children's attention to various aspects of a text so that in their future reading they become consciously aware of what the writer is doing.

Eventually, children can be encouraged to emulate in their own writing these wonderful and exciting ways of expression (Figure 2.3). The group construction of these particular elements – beginnings, endings, vivid passages, detailed information and so on – is a very effective workshop type activity, even with Y2 or Y3 children, in which half a dozen children co-operatively contribute to the composition and production of a text, continually rereading their efforts and improving upon them before deciding upon the final draft. Alongside these activities can run similar ones on an individual or paired basis, always with the teacher emphasising the need to reread and reform what is written.

In this type of activity, as well as learning to compose a text they are practising also their ability to reread the text as it emerges, reform parts of it and build up on it.

At a later stage, certainly at Y5 and Y6, a simple story frame can be used. Stein and Trabasso in 1982 suggested the following categories and types of causal relations occurring in a simple story.

Figure 2.3 *Is that what really happened?*

---

1 Setting Introduction of the protagonist; contains information about the social, physical or temporal context in which the story events occur.

Allow episode:
2 Initiating event An action, an internal event, or a physical event that serves to initiate the storyline or cause the protagonist to respond emotionally and to formulate a goal.

Cause:
3 Internal response An emotional reaction and a goal, often incorporating the thoughts of the protagonist that cause him to initiate action.

Cause:
4 Attempt An overt action or series of actions, carried out in the service of attaining the goal.

Cause or enable:
5 Consequence An event, action or end state, marking the attainment or non-attainment of the protagonist's goal.

Cause:
6 Reaction An internal response expressing the protagonist's feelings about the outcome of his actions or the occurrence of broader, general consequences resulting from the goal attainment of the protagonist.

This requires the writer to follow a prescribed pattern under a number of sub-headings; six in this case, although one or two of the sections can be omitted in certain circumstances. The teacher outlines the sub-headings and then proceeds to work out with the children possible responses to each stage in the frame and Stein and Trabasso give the following example of a well-formed story.

Setting	1 Once there was a big grey fish named Albert.
	2 He lived in a big icy pond near the edge of the forest.
Initiating event	3 One day, Albert was swimming round the pond.
	4 Then he spotted a big juicy worm on the top of the water.
Internal response	5 Albert knew how delicious worms tasted.
	6 He wanted to eat that one for his dinner.
Attempt	7 So he swam very close to the worm.
	8 Then he bit into him.
Consequence	9 Suddenly, Albert was pulled out of the water into a boat.
	10 He had been caught by a fisherman.
Reaction	11 Albert felt very sad.
	12 He wished he had been more careful.

Taken from Stein and Trabasso (1982), in R. Glaser (ed.) *Advances in Instructional Psychology*, Vol. 2. Hillsdale: Lawrence Erlbaum.

Once the children have participated with the teacher in composing a story that follows the story frame, they can with the help of guidance sheets produce stories of their own.

An adaptation of this by Roni Armstrong, a postgraduate student, during teaching practice with a Year 6 class in Claremont Junior School in Moss Side, Manchester, proved highly successful in producing some excellent texts and some highly critical reading. The work sheets she provided are shown in Figures 2.4 and 2.5.

These two activities alone – the use of models from literature and the use of a simple story frame – provide a high degree of involvement in reading, organising a text and evaluating what is written, so that reading becomes an increasingly critical activity.

What sort of reading lessons?

What should be the form, duration and frequency of reading lessons?

Naturally, the answer will depend upon the purpose of the session, but whatever this purpose, in the early stages lessons should be

AIM: To investigate the reason why some fabrics are waterproof, and some are not.

HYPOTHESIS: Think about our work last week – the differences in feel of nylon and cotton. Also, think about what is waterproof.

METHOD: What were you observing?

☆ REMEMBER TO LOOK AT THE FIBRES ☆

RESULTS: What happened when cotton had wax put on it? Did it change its feel?

CONCLUSION: Can you think why some textiles absorb water and others do not? Think about the feel of the textiles – did smooth textiles (or smooth fibres) absorb or repel water?

Figure 2.4

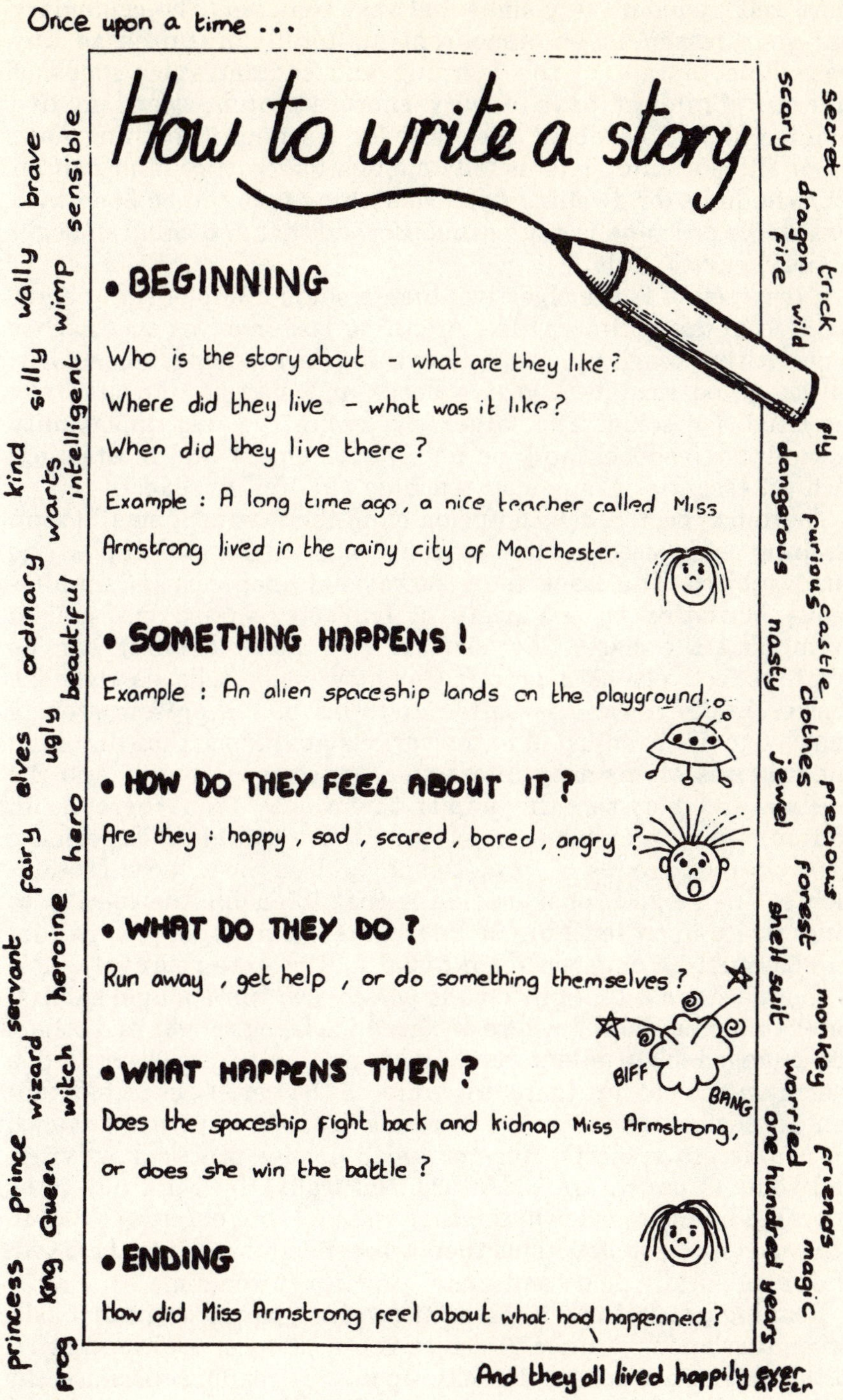

Once upon a time ...

How to write a story

• BEGINNING

Who is the story about — what are they like?
Where did they live — what was it like?
When did they live there?

Example : A long time ago, a nice teacher called Miss Armstrong lived in the rainy city of Manchester.

• SOMETHING HAPPENS !

Example : An alien spaceship lands on the playground.

• HOW DO THEY FEEL ABOUT IT ?

Are they : happy, sad, scared, bored, angry ?

• WHAT DO THEY DO ?

Run away, get help, or do something themselves ?

• WHAT HAPPENS THEN ?

Does the spaceship fight back and kidnap Miss Armstrong, or does she win the battle ?

BIFF   BANG

• ENDING

How did Miss Armstrong feel about what had happenned ?

And they all lived happily ever after.

Left margin words: brave wally silly sensible wimp intelligent warts kind ordinary beautiful ugly elves fairy servant wizard prince princess frog King Queen witch heroine hero fly

Right margin words: secret trick dragon scary wild fire furious castle dangerous clothes nasty jewel precious forest shell suit monkey friends magic worried one hundred years

Figure 2.5

short and frequent, very short and very frequent. The customary half-hour lesson is an anachronism, totally unsuited to any reasonable concept of the learning and concentration spans of children. Children have a very short attention span, so five minutes should be about the limit for learning something new; ten or fifteen minutes is usually enough for practice; and half an hour the limit for dwelling upon something that can be done with reasonable ease and is engrossing. Beyond that and children begin to look heavenwards!

If instruction is the objective, then a small group of six or eight children is the optimum size. Anything less involves the teacher in repetitive teaching, whilst anything larger tends to be less refined to particular children's needs and may be unnecessarily repetitive for some. The larger the group the less opportunity there is for feedback and for pupil involvement and interaction, each an essential element in teaching children to read.

There has been much confusion as to the merits of small group teaching as opposed to class teaching with all the children on the same subject. The issue here, however, is not various simultaneous activities on a variety of subjects versus one subject throughout the class. The issue is, how many children can be taught effectively as a group? Common sense tells us that the answer is the fewer the better in terms of the presentation of knowledge finely adjusted to the various abilities within the class, but in terms of ensuring interaction between the pupils and the teacher and between the pupils themselves then there is an optimum minimum below which interaction dwindles. Experience suggests that groups of three to six children meet these requirements. The second consideration is that to enable the teacher to concentrate upon teaching or interacting with a group, the other groups must be engaged upon tasks that require relatively little of the teacher's attention. This is possible within a single subject, for example in reading where one group is being taught and others are engaged upon silent reading, searching for words round a theme and so on, but there are limits to the variety of things that can be devised and it is much easier if the groups are engaged upon different subjects, some of which involve practical activities and some of which are sedentary. Naturally, the work has to be allocated by the teacher in the first instance, but once the children can read simple instructions then work sheets come into their own and, incidentally, form additional practice in reading.

Reading practice can be on an individual, paired or group basis, depending upon whether the objective is silent or oral reading. It is important not to dwell solely upon oral reading, because the ultimate objective is skilled silent reading. Therefore, time should be allocated every day for silent reading, and if this is frequently followed by asking the reader to recall the story orally or in writing, as appropriate, the exercise in the reconstruction of a message or story is good mental training as well as emphasising the need to read for meaning and for retention.

An effort should be made to arrange conditions for silent reading in school akin to those sought out by children in a comfortable home. Extra large cushions or extra thick foam placed in a book corner, help to create conditions conducive to pleasurable reading. There should be easy access to a range of books and insistence upon the desirability of undisturbed reading. Just as there is a psychological approach to selling by shopkeepers, so there is a psychological approach to inducing children to read.

Story-time

Story-time: of what should it consist?
Story-time should not be regarded as something that merely fills a gap at the end of a day, neither should it be placed invariably at the end of a morning or afternoon session.

Story-time can be the communal enjoyment of a piece of literature, including of course poetry. It can be the occasion for encountering a new word or phrase or experiencing a particular use of language, hence a flip chart should always be at hand upon which can be written new words and fresh language patterns. Illustrations, paintings, sketches and photographs can illuminate the text, but should be clearly displayed not flashed in a tantalising manner. All these activities widen the children's experiences, stimulate their thoughts and provoke oral responses.

There is, however, another purpose for reading to children. It is to convey to those children in the reception class who are not read to at home some idea of how to 'handle' a book and what can be obtained from it. In these sessions the teacher should not assume too readily that very young children, around the age of five, know what they can get from books or realise what they are getting from them. Therefore, it is essential to talk with the children about the books that are about to be read to them and about the story as it unfolds. It will also be necessary to show children where one starts and how one proceeds to read a book, and for this purpose a very small group of children at a time can stand behind the teacher looking over the shoulder, listening and watching what the teacher does. They will see where reading begins, follow the teacher's finger as it points periodically to the lines that are being read, and in this way gradually learn that print proceeds from top to bottom and left to right. The uninitiated will learn gradually that the reader gets a message from

Figure 2.6 'And that was an unexpected thing to happen.'

the printed text rather than simply from the illustrations. These are difficult concepts for a very young naive child, but there is no better way of experiencing them than by watching and experiencing an adult reading aloud.

There is also a deeper significance in reading to children, that emerged from the research of Gordon Wells (1987) in Bristol. This suggested that it affords the opportunity for them to experience a variety of language structures in engrossing situations, and it introduces an abstract element into their thinking, taking the children's thoughts beyond their immediate experiences and environment.

Word study and comprehension

What about word study and comprehension in the later stages of reading development?
Word study and comprehension were regarded in the past as separate things when discussing the development of reading

skills. Now it is realised that they are inextricably interwoven. Words form the basis of meaning and it is their arrangement that affects the precise meaning that they convey. *The boy bit the dog* is very different from *The dog bit the boy*, although the words are identical and the action similar. It is the particular arrangement that conveys the exact meaning. Even where words have more than one meaning – such as the word *bear* which can refer to an animal, or an action on the Stock Exchange, or it can mean to carry something – the exact meaning can be picked out as a result of the syntactic and semantic cues that surround the word: the *grizzly bear*, the *market was bearish, the pain was hard to bear*. Thus, in order to understand any text it is necessary to be able to recognise the words, to appreciate the significance of their grammatical arrangement and to be familiar with the particular structure to be read. For example, in the following two sentences: *The heinous crime was committed by the miscreant after the hostelry closed its doors*, and *The heinous crime, committed by the miscreant after the hostelry closed its doors*, the reader must know the meaning of *miscreant* and *hostelry*, while the word *heinous* can be guessed in all probability. However, the reader must know also that both sentences mean the same thing, except that in the case of the second sentence the punctuation indicates that something further is to be added about the heinous crime.

This illustrates the importance of exposing children frequently, over a long period of time, to a variety of language structures and patterns, something that is most effectively started by reading good literature to them from as early an age as possible.

However, it is not only familiarity with words and with language structures that enable a child to understand a text. There must exist or develop an ability and a disposition to process what is being read in an additional way: that is, semantically. The reader must build up the message of the text from the words and structures, reflecting upon them and reformulating them into a manageable body of knowledge.

Naturally, this can be done most effectively if the reader is unimpeded by word recognition difficulties and has been trained to reflect upon and reformulate the thoughts he gets from the text. This means there must be constant challenges to readers to build up a wide vocabulary and to increase their familiarity with a wide range of language structures that can best be acquired in two ways. One way is through challenges to express orally and in writing new ideas, or old ideas in new guises. Group composition of texts to meet a variety of audiences can be very productive of both new words and new structures, especially if the teacher plays a participatory role. The other, complementary way, is through reading. Time should be set aside every day for silent private reading in the junior classes, and these sessions should lead to small group discussions that arise out of the stories read or the information gathered. The crucial thing is that there must be some outcome from oral and written composition and reading in order to ensure that children acquire the habit of reflection. Reflection fosters comprehension.

Some writers have advocated exercises in quicker reading at the junior stage on two counts. Quicker reading makes processing the input from the text easier. The reader can 'package' the information so that it is more easily retained in the short-term memory and transferred effectively to the long-term memory. The other reason is that such exercises are another way of showing a reader how to make optimum use of a text, such as a book, with the minimum of effort.

Finally, if it is done well, poetry reading and writing make an excellent vehicle for the study of words and for practice in their usage. Words have to be found to 'fit' in terms of meaning and in terms of their sound or number of syllables. At its best, it can require a high degree of competence in searching the memory for words, and in reading poetry, unusual language structures alert the reader to the possibilities of language. Again it must be stressed that greater understanding of texts will come through greater involvement in the creation of texts. If you are practised in something then you are better equipped to understand it, in the sense that a lawyer must practise law in order fully to appreciate its consequences.

Reading for slow learners

What should be done for children who find it difficult to learn to read?

In approaching this problem it must be accepted that children learn at different paces. Some realise what is involved in learning to read before they enter school, some for one reason or another, and there are several possibilities, do not learn the 'trick' until they are well into the junior school.

One thing is certain, however, and that is that the slower learners still need to go through, in one form or another, the programme that is outlined in Chapter 3, and if at any stage in that programme they are found to be faltering, that is the optimum moment for remedial measures to be employed, and not later, in the junior classes, when they have suffered years of indignity. Their difficulties should not be ignored in the hope that they will be remedied at a later stage. The purpose of continuous assessment is to avoid failure by continuously taking remedial measures where necessary. In many cases, the causes of failure begin in a very small way: a child misses a week's teaching at a crucial stage, or misunderstands some aspect of learning to read because the proper behaviour needed to learn a particular process has not been acquired.

This argues strongly for seriously executed continuous assessment, and for periods of intensive remedial measures whenever appropriate. It means also that programmes of teaching children to read should not be implemented as though all the children was capable of learning at the same pace. Plans should be made that take into account the fact that some children will take much longer than others to learn to read. These children should not be ignored: the programme must be paced to coincide with the capabilities of the learners.

Unfortunately, this does not always happen and children with reading difficulties are found in classes Y5 and Y6. They cannot be taken at a normal pace through the programme in the same way as successful or even moderately achieving children. What they need is a 'crash' programme – a programme divided into frequently occurring short intensive periods covering the fundamental issues in learning to read. These are: the visual recognition and identification of letter clusters; the acquisition of a reserve of immediately recognisable words (both G. and J. Underwood and Professor Hazel Francis have stressed this crucial element in reading skill); and teaching that shows them how, rather than merely expecting them, to gain this knowledge and use it. In its simplest terms, it means showing the children how the teacher splits up words, associates sounds with the parts and then blends together the parts, and in doing so searches for meaning. Similarly, in reading a text, teachers must show the children how to read prose, not word by word but in phrases so that meaning emerges (Perera, 1989).

Much of this can be done effectively through a programme of instruction in spelling and writing, so that the children learn to construct words and compose texts. They need more instruction in spelling of the kind which emphasises pronounceable units, and they need to be induced to reflect more consciously upon what they write; they need this in short intensive periods of ten minutes duration; and they need these periods frequently – several times per day over half a term at the minimum. This can be done within the literacy hour to a certain extent, but it would be reasonable to intrude into periods outside the literacy hour in the case of children who require intensive remedial reinforcement of what they have learned in the literacy hour. The reason for this concentrated effort is that progress must be seen and felt by the children so that their aspirations are raised. Furthermore, frequency reduces 'forgetting' time in the intervals between learning sessions.

A 'crash' programme that meets these requirements, of involvement in spelling and writing, is intensive for short periods, and can involve half a dozen to a dozen children working simultaneously, is one that was proposed by an American psychologist, Grace Fernald. Under her scheme children with experience of failure in learning to read are remotivated by the teacher proving to them that they can learn to spell, and thereby to recognise, any word that they choose. This is done by the teacher writing out the word in large script, and then tracing over it with the forefinger while pronouncing the syllables. The children must then emulate this procedure of tracing and vocalisation for as many times as it takes to be able to write the word without copying. With success in this initial activity, the children can then proceed to write any story or piece of information that they please, asking the teacher for any word that they think they cannot spell. The teacher writes the word, traces and pronounces it, then the child traces and pronounces the word several times – at least six times and usually more – and checks that learning has taken place by writing the word without copying. The child can then proceed to compile the text until another word is reached that cannot be spelt, when the above procedure is repeated.

When the writing is completed, the teacher types or rewrites a correct version. This is done overnight, and the next day the child reads the correct version of the text aloud to the teacher. Any words that were spelt incorrectly are then learned properly, and all the words asked for by the child are retained as a list to be revised weekly during the period of the programme. Hence, there is no escape!

Interspersed with this writing, the children choose any reading books from a wide array, ask the teacher for any unrecognised words which are then written on a book marker and pronounced by the teacher and, at the end of the chapter, learned by the tracing, vocalisation and writing-without-copying routine. These words are also revised weekly.

The teacher will have commented upon the structure of the words that are asked for by the children and will have drawn comparisons with similarly constructed words previously learned. During the week, after the completion of the writing and reading of the stories written, time will be set aside for further discussion about the structure and meaning of the words learned, the further drawing of comparisons, and the searching for other words that bear comparison in some way with those learned. These words in turn will be placed in context with regard to meaning and then learned by the tracing, vocalisation and writing-without-copying method. Children will be encouraged to categorise these words into a vocabulary collection based on corresponding elements within the words. For example, words which begin or end with a common blend, which contain a common letter string or syllable such as *-able, -gh, -ght,* which have a common ending such as *-ious, -tion, -ing, -aneous,* which have a common sound but a different meaning, and words that are related to a specific subject or were used in a particular story. In this way words will frequently appear in more than one category. This will help the children to recall these words by association. The one thing that must not be done is to place these words in a collection and then forget about them. This was frequently the disadvantage of the old idea of a personal spelling book. Once the teacher had written the word no further reference was made to it with the result that children often requested words to be spelt for them which were already entered in their spelling book. The habit of searching for words previously encountered should be firmly established, and the children who meticulously follow this line should be enthusiastically praised for this is an aspect of training in reflection and in conscious attempts to recall previously learned material, all part of learning to learn.

The advantages of this method are many. It is different from the usual methods upon which the child has failed; it is engrossing because it is activity-based and the child has to give attention to words, if only to follow the letters with the forefinger; and it is not abstract in that it is a constructional activity rather than one that entails observation which can easily become passive. It contains all the ingredients of the programme suggested for normally progressing children: it involves letter recognition and formation, analysis of words into syllabic units and the synthesis of those units and it involves the teacher in continuously showing how this should be done. It ensures concentration, application and reflection on the part of the learner, and it provides reading practice using known material, so that a natural reading pose is easily adopted in order to convey meaning. Just like the Reading Recovery System of Marie Clay, it provides one to one teaching between teacher and child, but, unlike the extortionately expensive Reading Recovery approach, it can be carried out as a group method within a class of normal size employing one teacher for the whole class. Indeed, it was used very successfully in one reported piece of research with a Y6 class of thirty-seven children, seventeen of whom had reading ages of six and below.

This is a programme that fits nicely into the National Curriculum, covering all aspects of English: spoken language, reading, writing, spelling and handwriting.

Finally, the topics children choose to write about will arise frequently out of children's particular interests and will be prepared orally in small-group or teacher-child discussion. Children can be encouraged also to retell stories that have been read to them – a useful activity in the reconstruction of thoughts and in the type of writing that Bereiter and Scardamalia call 'knowledge telling'.

Reading Recovery: a pointer to the future?

Reading Recovery (Clay, 1993), on the other hand, is not intended for general use by a class teacher. It is intended solely for use by a specially trained teacher working with one child at a time. The child is selected as failing after one year in school and is then comprehensively assessed in an attempt to discover the difficulties that the child is having. Based on this assessment a programme is composed which attempts to rectify the deficiencies in the child's approach to learning to read over a period of twelve to twenty weeks, during which time teacher and child spend thirty minutes together each school day. These half-hour periods are intensive and move at a brisk pace.

A typical lesson 'would include each of these activities, usually in the following order, as the format of the daily lesson:

- rereading two or more familiar books   text
- rereading yesterday's new book and taking a
  running record   text
- letter identification (plastic letters on a magnetic   words and
  board) and/or word-making and breaking   letters
- writing a story (including hearing and recording   text
  sounds in words)   sounds
- cut-up story to be rearranged   text
- new book introduced   text
- new book attempted   text

. . . individual variations in lesson plans are always possible, providing there is a sound rationale based on a particular child's response to lessons' (Clay, 1993).

The programmes which vary from child to child will be designed specifically to overcome 'sticking points' in the child's acquisition of reading skills. Therefore, although such a programme will, of necessity have to cover all the major elements in a normal programme of teaching children to read, it will pay particular and special attention to those elements that are deemed to be causing problems for the particular child. In other words Reading Recovery is a development of an approach advocated by Marion Monroe (*Children Who Cannot Read*, 1932) in which a profile of errors was compiled for each failing child and a suitably pointed remedial programme was drawn up. The difference between the two schemes is that Reading Recovery requires an enormous input by the teacher, who is continually searching for techniques which prove successful. It is based upon an enlightened approach through children's literature involving a great deal of interaction between child, teacher and subject matter. The Monroe proposals did not have this attractive pedagogical approach.

Furthermore, in the Reading Recovery programme writing plays an important role in providing the child with an active insight into the composition of texts. In this way it follows the example of Fernald (1943) and is in line with normal practice in schools, whereby writing and spelling play their part in the reading programme.

Hurry (1996) gives several reasons for the success of Reading Recovery: intensity of intervention by the teacher; rigour and focus of assessment; breadth of curriculum for reading which includes writing as well as reading; and the quality of instruction. To these are added the facts that children are taught to adopt self-correcting strategies when attempting to read new material; that 'phonic skills are addressed directly, but always in the context of the child's reading or the child's writing'; and that the teachers, who have been through the rigorous training provided by Reading Recovery tutors, have a deep understanding of their subject matter and their role.

There is sufficient evidence here to assert that Reading Recovery in theory makes useful and important suggestions which are crucial in teaching children to read: namely, the need for more able teachers who have an understanding of the structure of language, and who have received specialist training in child psychology, learning theory and assessment as well as in flexible techniques of teaching; the advantage of the early identification of children who are experiencing difficulties in order to avoid the development of what John Merritt (1972) termed 'reading neurosis' – the fear of further failure; that teaching should encompass more than imparting knowledge, it should show children how to use their knowledge and how to circumvent gaps in knowledge, such as learning a complex and irregularly spelt word by heart rather than continuing to stumble in its analysis; and, finally, that the child should not be diverted from the main task of learning to read through an over-emphasis on 'pictorial material or puzzles but will be taught what he needs to learn in the context of continuous text' (Clay, 1993). However, given the financial constraints of the education budget Reading Recovery in its practical application of one teacher per failing child cannot hope to do all that is necessary to ensure that all children meet the assessment levels required by the National Curriculum. Nevertheless, much can be learned from the Reading Recovery programme, and many of its strategies incorporated by the class teacher into more general approaches, such as that by Fernald described above, when dealing with the less able children in the class.

Is assessment necessary?

Is assessment necessary and, if so, what form should it take?

Assessment is not merely necessary, it is vital. If a teacher does not know what a child knows, how can that child be taught effectively? Assessment enables decisions to be made concerning the effectiveness of the teaching in terms of the learning that has taken place. It also allows teachers to make decisions that determine the form that any subsequent teaching should take. Thus in assessing what children have learned and the degree to which the learning has been effective, teachers are able to reflect upon their teaching techniques and thereby make any necessary adjustments to those techniques as they proceed. Hence, the assessment of children should be regarded as a form of self-evaluation by teachers. It is without doubt an inherent element in teaching.

The form of the assessment will vary according to the task that is being assessed. Essentially, it must be a means of checking children's accomplishments in the process of learning to read and it must be seen as a vehicle for the evaluation of teaching techniques. For example, if a child has been taught the word *cat*, the teacher will want to know whether, when confronted by the printed word *cat*, the child responds to the correct oral form; if not, then the teacher will want to consider how he or she went about teaching that word and whether or not it could have been presented in a different and more effective manner. The teacher may have presented it as *ca-t*, which eases pronunciation but which as a discrete exercise does not call up so readily in the child's mind words learned previously and ending in *at*, and from which a correct response to *cat* can be derived. On the other hand, the child may have had some words beginning with *ca* on a recent occasion and simply needs to be reminded of them in order to activate a response to the new word *cat*. Even teachers with a wealth of experience cannot always anticipate precisely the optimum techniques or approaches to use on every occasion with every child. Therefore, on the basis of continuous assessment, they have to make readjustments resulting from reflection upon the child's responses and upon a consideration of the alternative teaching techniques and approaches that are available.

It is upon this dual role of assessment – as a check upon learning and as a challenge to teacher reflection and versatility – that assessment in the National Curriculum is based. Throughout the period of Key Stage 1, covering the early stages of learning to read, teachers are required to cover the standards of attainment set down (these are an indication of the sub-skills and behaviours that have to be acquired in learning to read) and to assess how effectively this has been accomplished. Hence they are assessing the progress of the children and as a consequence they are in a position to evaluate their own teaching techniques. And if this assessment, followed by evaluation, is pursued diligently in relation to all the teaching that is done in the English Curriculum, including writing and spelling, then it is virtually inevitable that teaching standards will be raised.

It is important to keep in mind when you are following the *Assessment Handbook for English in the National Curriculum* the argument made in this book that writing, spelling and handwriting all contribute to the development of reading skill. Attempts to formulate the letters of the alphabet, to spell words and to compose texts all contribute to a child's awareness of various aspects of reading. Thus, in learning to recognise a word, attempts to spell it, write it and to experience it in its context will all contribute significantly to a successful outcome. Therefore, reading and its assessment cannot be seen in isolation. When a child is being taught and assessed in spelling, he is in fact being taught and assessed in an aspect of reading.

It is for these reasons that students should be wary of reading the Programmes of Study for the National Curriculum as though they are separate entities for reading, writing, spelling and handwriting. They are presented separately for clarity and to avoid omission. For teaching purposes, they need to be integrated or at least regarded as strongly interrelated.

Assessment in the National Curriculum

In what ways do the assessment requirements of the National Curriculum affect teaching techniques?
The objective of the assessment programme is to ensure that relevant facts are learnt and necessary processes and behaviours are acquired. These include: the recognition and identification of words, including the letters of the alphabet and their sounds, and the acquisition of word attack skills; the awareness of the nature of text and the use of phono-graphemic, syntactic (grammatical)

and semantic cues in the interpretation of texts; the exercise of thought processes in the comprehension of texts; and, the use of books for pleasure and as a source for information. Admittedly, the form of the assessment programme changed in 1994 so that in Key Stage 1 it takes the form of teacher assessment and listening to children reading at Levels 1 and 2 and of tests of reading comprehension at Levels 3 and 4. However, this does not alter the nature of the approach or the coverage of the skills. Letter identification, word recognition and comprehension of texts and all that is involved in comprehension are covered. Thus what is needed is a teaching programme that covers all these aspects, and approaches them from the various angles of spelling, writing, handwriting, and reading itself.

Grafted onto this teaching and assessment programme should be a conscious effort on the part of teachers to take the matter further, beyond simply checking responses, so that some deeper understanding of the children's responses is gained. An instance where this can be done is at Level 2 where teachers are expected to mark a running record of children's reading.

This procedure is based on Miscue Analysis (Goodman, 1969), which has been adapted for use in classrooms in Britain by Arnold (1982), and which with further amendment is offered as a teaching technique in the section, *Miscue analysis and listening to children read*, on page 49. Goodman suggested that a child's response to an obstacle encountered when reading gives an indication of the thought process involved and the type of cues being employed. He termed the actual response a 'miscue'. For example, when confronted with the initial sentence in a text, *The boy walked up to the house on the hill*, if the reader's response is, *The boy walked up to his* home *on the hill*, it can be assumed that his response to the word *house* indicates both carelessness and understanding, while the supplementing of *the* with *his* suggests an as yet unjustified assumption.

The conclusions to be drawn from this are that the reader is developing some perfectly acceptable and admirable reading behaviours, in that interpretation and anticipation are playing a prominent part. Semantic and syntactic cues are being employed to the full. However, there is less than full attention being given to a discerning use of phono-graphemic cues, and it may indicate a deficiency in the knowledge of some phono-graphemic correspondences – he may not know how to respond to the digraph *ou* in *house* and therefore relies solely upon the cue *h* to fit in a likely response given the semantic and syntactic cues that he so readily employs.

Hence in this case there are indications that some attention to the phonic analysis of certain words is called for together with some further training in attention to the details of words whilst reading. Admittedly, skilled readers can pay scant attention to many words in the texts that they read, but then they have acquired a sensitivity to the possibilities of miscuing and they automatically check their anticipation against the text where necessary.

Full details of a modified form of miscue analysis for use in classrooms, rather than a tool in clinical analysis, are given by Arnold (1982), *Listening to Children Reading*. As indicated in the title, the object of miscue analysis is to listen to children read and to draw conclusions from their responses that will help in formulating subsequent teaching strategies with a particular reader or with a group of readers who display common deficiencies in their reading. Several important pointers of general guidance affecting teaching strategies will emerge from a study of miscue analysis and the ideas of Goodman. The first develops from Goodman's insistence that the actual analysis of a child's reading should not begin immediately the child begins to read the passage. It should begin when the child is some way into the text, so that when the analysis itself begins, the reader will have gained some idea of the message. This will remind teachers of the importance of meaning in the interpretation of texts. It also implies the importance of anticipatory behaviours on the part of the reader, and it is a reminder that anticipatory thoughts whilst reading are something to be encouraged and controlled. For example, anticipation will and should run high with an opening to a text of *The naughty little boy found the yoghurt very . . .* However, some degree of control and care is required in identifying the appropriate choice of word which completes the sentence: *The naughty little boy found the yoghurt very tasty*, because the reader may dislike yoghurt and may be so sure that the final word will reflect his own thoughts about yoghurt that he will rely upon reduced cues provided by the letter string, *asty*, and consequently his miscue will be /næsti:/ rather than the actual word /teisti:/.

In such a case it would be advisable for the teacher to expect the child to read the next sentence, *He would have liked more, but . . .* and then for the teacher to confront him with his response to the word *tasty*, and thereby expect the child to reflect more closely upon what he has read and to check the actual word which carried the miscue.

In this simple instance of a single miscue the opportunity arose for teaching that encouraged reflection upon the complete text, an activity that improves comprehension (Lunzer and Gardner, 1979), and provided additionally the opportunity for instruction about word attack skills, which Francis (1982) and G. and J. Underwood (1986) imply are crucially important because their findings showed that a major deficiency in poor readers was an inability to recognise a substantial proportion of words in a text. This was an ideal situation in which a reader was challenged to use phono-graphemic, syntactic (grammatical) and semantic cues. Phonic analysis was practised within a meaningful context and a full range of reading behaviours was exercised.

Another element in miscue analysis requires the reader to retell what he has read. This provides evidence of the degree of understanding gained by the reader from the text. It has the additional benefit of impressing upon the child, in a very practical way, the need to make a conscious effort whilst reading to understand and to retain what is read. It is too easy for children to become thoughtless, or rather careless, readers, content to read the words, momentarily get the message, but not really to absorb that message. Reading is a tool for learning, and learning requires effort on the part of the learner, as we all know.

The proposals for testing at Key Stage 2 are similar in form to those for Key Stage 1 (1994). Hence the running record of children's errors whilst reading will reveal any deficiencies in the use of phono-graphemic, syntactic and semantic cues. This requirement is a strong indicator that the teaching of reading must play an important part at Key Stage 2. The test of comprehension will present a strong pointer to the need for children to practise reading a variety of texts and for teachers to give training in the interpretation of those texts. Such tests of writing and spelling will ensure a more rigorous approach to the composition of texts, and consequently to an understanding of them. Needless to say the current documents of the National Curriculum Council must be studied carefully as it is the responsibility of teachers to execute them strictly in accordance with the Council's instructions.

It is also necessary to be wary of treating the results of the kind of testing advocated by the National Curriculum Council as a foolproof indicator of absolute standards. Evidence has emerged from research by Julie Davies of the Centre for Primary Education in the University of Manchester that the results of the National Curriculum tests do not necessarily coincide with those of standardised tests. For example, it was found that whereas the National Curriculum tests on Year 6 children found girls outperforming boys, the standardised tests showed no statistically significant differences between boys and girls on the reading measure. Davies concludes, 'assessment is clearly a very complex activity which can easily produce invalid data. This should be borne in mind when national test results are relied on so heavily in any debate on standards'.

The implications for teachers are that they should be meticulous in applying the national tests and that they should be aware of the fallibility of non-standardised tests. The latter can easily be 'adjusted' to meet the exigencies of fraught situations.

Miscue analysis and listening to children read

Can miscue analysis be simplified further for use in everyday teaching?

Very effective use can be made of the findings of a miscue analysis in a simplified form, provided the types of miscue – Non-response (refusal), Substitution, Omission, Insertion, Reversal, Self-correction, Hesitation and Repetition – *are interpreted in terms of deficiencies of factual knowledge* and *inappropriate behaviours whilst reading*. The following work sheet is offered as an exemplar.

Using miscue analysis as a teaching device

The teacher must have a double-spaced copy of the text which can be marked in the following way:

1 Encircle omissions: word, syllable, letter string or letter.
2 Insert a ⟨ sign plus word for all insertions.
3 Underline and write in all mispronunciations.
4 Draw a line through words for which substitutions were made and write in the substitution.
5 Use a wavy line to indicate repetitions.
6 Use a dotted line to indicate hesitations.

There should be a few sentences to be read by way of introduction to the part of the text that is to be marked.

Example of a marked script

	Miscue
Spot was⟨a⟩good dog. He never ran after	1
the saw	
⟨*boys and girls or cars. But Woof* ~~was~~ *a*	2 3
boys	
naughty dog. He ran after ~~dogs~~ *and*	4
and	
girl's⟨*horses and cars and he barked*	5 6 7
at ⟨*all of*⟩*them*	8

Interpretation of miscues with teacher responses in brackets
Miscue number

1 Syntactic-grammatical mistake. (Challenge child to say whether the sentence as read sounds right.)
2 Acceptable insertion. (Refer back to it later.)
3 Misinterpretation of graphic sequence. (Phonic prompting needed in reassessing the word and further phonic training.)
4 Probably reading ahead – 'boys and girls'. Good reading behaviour in one respect, but defective in failing to check anticipatory thoughts against phonic cues. (Get child to reread and to take special notice of every word. Further practice necessary in forward and backward cueing.)
5 Insertion indicating unawareness of the apostrophe. (Brief explanation pending fuller instruction about the significance of the apostrophe.)
6 Repetition of words both previously read in line two, because child sees a difficult word – *barked* – appearing as child reads ahead. (Not an unreasonable miscue as the reader is displaying a characteristic feature of skilled reading, namely, reading ahead.)
7 Hesitation, probably indicating unsureness about the word *barked*. (Phonic guidance necessary concerning the manageable boundaries within the word – *bar-k-ed*.)
8 Omission which is acceptable because the sense is retained. (Merely comment on omission.)

This use of miscues as a basis for instruction was used successfully in reading clinics directed by the author in a summer school at the State University of New York at Albany in 1976 and has since been used intermittently by students practising in English schools.

This type of activity should occur frequently as it gives a greater sense of purpose to the act of listening to children read. Once marked the sheets can be retained and, when four or more have been assembled, a profile of each child's errors can be drawn up showing where further teaching and practice are necessary.

Continuous assessment of this intensity will ensure continuing refinement of teaching techniques and adjustments of the programme of study to the needs of the children.

IT and reading and writing

What part can IT play in teaching children to read and write?
One thing that has been stressed throughout this book is the need to get children so engrossed in activity with language, words and letters that they will feel impelled to experiment in the

construction of words and the composition of texts, and that they will do so in a probing, hypothesis-testing and flexible manner. They must feel free to experiment, and they must see immediately the results of their experimentation. Word processors can provide an alternative form of experimentation to those normally associated with reading and writing.

There is something compelling in the desire of children to play with and operate machines. The computer has the advantage of being a machine that can be used as a tool for the purposes of learning to read, write and spell.

First, there is the keyboard and the opportunities it presents for familiarisation with letter shapes. This can, after an initial start with pencil and paper, soon lead on to exploratory or invented spelling and writing, when children pretend to spell and to write. These activities should never be regarded as a replacement for using pencil and paper, which provide opportunities for learning through the tactile and kinaesthetic senses, but simply as a additional motivator and form of practice. It is possible to learn the letters of the alphabet by looking at them and selecting them on a keyboard, but to draw the letters with a pencil impresses the letter form upon the memory more effectively.

Secondly, programs with a voice output provide facilities for reading practice similar to those provided by the talking book.

Thirdly, the word processor is a useful aid to composing a written text. An array of ideas can be displayed that can subsequently be re-sorted and redrafted – another form of sequencing activity. Words, phrases, sentences and paragraphs can be moved around with ease. There are programs in which a word bank can be called up on a variety of topics, so that children have at their finger tips a range of words from which to select the most appropriate. And in terms of presentation, the spelling check facility is invaluable. The only danger with the latter is that it can cut out an awareness in a child of spelling problems that need rectifying.

Thus the word processor can be used as a constructional tool for familiarisation with letters, the construction of words and the composition of texts, including design and presentation. As such, it can be used extensively by children, but it cannot replace the teacher's efforts to inculcate the essential behaviours that are necessary in learning to read.

It is not possible within the confines of this short book to deal with the increasing number of software programmes that are available as aids. However, teachers will be interested in such software as *Tray, Fun with Text, Expose, Wordplay* to mention a few that can be used as aids to reading instruction, and in programmes that create a purposeful context for reading, such as

Toyshop, Elmtree Farm, Our School, Albert's House, Spot, and *Moving in*. All have found favour in schools.

Concluding response

Throughout the above responses you will have noted the following basic points:

1 the need to start with what children know, think or say and gradually to show how print can be attached to the letter names they know, the words they say or think of, and the thoughts they have;

2 the advantages of showing children how to look at words and how to create in them a disposition for seeking the boundaries within words: letters, letter strings, syllables and morphemes;

3 that the creation of this disposition for searching behaviour is dependent upon teachers encouraging children to be flexible and to experiment confidently with what they know when trying to decode words;

4 the advantages of spelling and writing, in that these activities serve to elucidate and clarify how words and texts are constructed, thereby helping the reader to more fully and more sensitively understand both the decoding of words and the comprehension of texts;

5 that in teaching children to read, the teacher must teach facts, inculcate understanding of the processes in which those facts are used, and instil a range of behaviours that enable the readers to use all the cues that are available to them, such as phonic cues, syntactic cues and semantic cues, knowing full well that all of them play a part in the comprehension of a text;

6 that the acquisition of a vocabulary of recognisable words sufficient to enable fluent reading, and the inculcation of reading behaviours such as association, searching and reflection, can only be accomplished over a longish period of time, during which frequency and reinforcement of learning are key factors in success.

These points form the basis from which a programme for teaching reading can be formulated. The contents of that programme are clearly defined; it is their interpretation and implementation that will vary according to the experience and ability of the children and the philosophy and skills of the teachers.

Teachers should always be prepared to make adjustments to any prepared scheme as evidence emerges of the needs of the particular children who are being taught.

3 A basic programme for teaching children to read

A point that cannot be over-emphasised is the importance of oral language in learning to read, spell and write. Attention to it should be an integral part of every step in a child's development. Not only must children develop a facility in the use of language for various purposes, they must become increasingly conscious of what they are doing. Halliday (1975) in *Learning How to Mean* reminds us of the various functions that form the basis of language usage:

- Instrumental – 'I want' – to obtain goods and services
- Regulatory – 'do as I tell you' – to control the behaviour of others
- Interactional – 'me and you' – to interact with others
- Personal – 'here I come' – expressions of feelings, interest, pleasure
- Heuristic – 'tell me why' – quest for knowledge
- Imaginative – 'let's pretend' – exploring and creating a universe
- Informative – 'I'll tell you' – informing and instructing.

The modern infant classroom, where children are engaged and engrossed in a variety of purposeful activities, is the ideal environment in which spoken language can be practised. It is also one in which teachers and auxiliaries can participate orally in order to guide, stimulate and provoke the use of appropriate forms of speech. Incorrect or inappropriate usage can be corrected within a context that ensures that the corrected form is appreciated, for teachers should not hesitate to explain the correction, emphasising and illustrating the difference between the correct and incorrect forms, so that the child not only understands what should have been said but in addition becomes familiar with the teacher's language of instruction.

This guided adjustment to the language of instruction centred upon activities such as sand and water play, art, technology and dramatic play forms a basis for gradual adjustment by the child to the language used by teachers when they are teaching children to read, spell and write. Such language not only has its own vocabulary with specific meanings, such as *word, letter* and *sound* when referring to a response to print, but it also has its own registers and patterns as in 'Tell me what you did' when we really mean 'Write down what you did'. In order to fully understand what the teacher is saying, the child must become familiar with the vocabulary, register and language patterns used by the teacher. This can only be achieved if the children begin to use similar forms of oral language themselves, and for that to happen teaching should involve, whenever possible, genuine attempts at discussion. It is not enough simply to talk at children; to engage them in discussion is an important first principle in teaching.

The programme that is outlined below is in a loose chronological order. A more precise prescription cannot be given because many activities persist in varying forms throughout the programme. An instance of this is word recognition. It begins in a very general form with the identification of familiar simple words and then proceeds with unfamiliar words until eventually somewhat esoteric words of a complex nature are encountered. This should be borne in mind when reading through the programme.

Another very important point to keep in mind whilst reading through this programme is that adjustments will be necessary to meet the varying needs of children at different stages of development and from varying backgrounds, including their previous classroom experiences.

Moreover, the classroom environment and the place of books and reading in that environment are crucial to the success of the programme. The environment for reading must be comfortable, the reading corner and class library inviting and reading by the teacher and eventually by the children must be a central feature of the school day in both infant and junior classes (Figure 3.1).

A reading programme

The alphabet: an easy introductory activity

Children upon entry into the reception class should be introduced to alphabet books and cards and there should be frequent references to the letters that go with the illustrations. Many children want to learn to read on their first day at school and beginning to get to know the alphabet is, amongst other things, a nice sop to this desire. It gives them something positive that they and their parents will appreciate. Chanting the names of the letters of the alphabet can be introduced. Some will know them, others will take some time,

Figure 3.1 *Learning to relax and enjoy reading is an essential aspect of the programme.*

six months or a year in some cases, to grasp them. Remember that success is important at all stages in learning to read, but at this very early stage it is imperative that the children do not feel under any threat or pressure. Chanting is something to be enjoyed in short, frequent spells. I-spy games calling the name of the object or animal will draw attention to the letters incidentally, and the children can match wooden cut-out letters to the printed form. After sufficient experiences children can try to trace the letters with their forefingers.

Initially children are taught to recognise and name the letters of the alphabet because it is an easy way to introduce children to the simplest feature of text. The letters are distinctive and require an easy-to-say label in order that by means of rote learning even the youngest children in the primary school can become familiar with them. In the process of doing this teachers can introduce children to words in the knowledge that the children will have been prepared to look, admittedly very hazily at first, at the components of words. Through this preparatory work with the alphabet, the children will have something to look for and to identify in words. Furthermore if the letters are presented repeatedly and accompanied by a picture and different word which varies with each presentation, so that the letter *b* is accompanied by *b*: b*a*t + drawing, *b*: b*u*n + drawing, *b*: b*o*at + drawing and so on, then children will learn also that each letter has one sound, or in some cases two sounds, which can be attached to it within the total sound of a word.

At first words with a corresponding initial letter will be used because the initial sound of a word is the most noticeable sound. However, soon words with a corresponding final sound will be introduced: *t* in b*at*, r*at*, p*it*, b*oat*, c*oat*. Not only does this alert children to the fact that letters make up words, it also begins their training in looking at all parts of a word and not concentrating solely on the initial part of it.

Once upon a time work of this nature was considered tedious because it was repetitive and required a purely visual-oral response, with teachers playing little part in the exercise except to require a response from the children. However, now the importance of context has been recognised as well as that of the interaction between teachers and children and of some form of active involvement on the part of children. Hence, a pattern emerges closely linked to the cyclic process of teaching which is explained in Chapter 5 and which can be embedded in the literacy hour. It could run something like this:

- A target letter is selected, say *b*, and the teacher begins by talking about a bear called Teddy and encourages the children to join in with statements about their teddies. There will be an illustration of a teddy bear and, possibly, a picture of real bears. The teacher writes the word *bear* on the blackboard and places alongside it a letter *b*. The children are asked to trace in the air a letter *b* following the teacher's actions.
- The teacher reads the story of *The Three Bears*. Every time the word *bear* in the story is heard the children, all of whom have a card with the word *bear* printed on it, raise the card, encouraged by the teacher. Such active involvement ensures greater attention during a story with which the children are familiar.
- The children are then required, individually, to place the letter *b* over the initial letter of the word *bear* on the cards they hold, and are encouraged to say the word *bear* with emphasis on the initial letter. In a subsequent lesson they could be required to select the letter *b* from an array of letters – not too many letters at first. Similarly, the word card *bear* would be selected from a choice of words.
- Various activities could follow: finger tracing the letter on the desk top or in a paint tray; handling a wooden cut-out form of the letter (a very important activity in terms of learning, especially if the letters are of wood, which is more substantial and more tactile than plastic); over-writing the letter

(beginnings of handwriting); and even attempts to write the letter, because although the result may only be scribble, this in itself is an important stage in learning to write. All these activities should involve discussions between teacher and children and should be accompanied by the teacher's involvement in the activities, because children learn from seeing how adults do things.

- Provided there has been sufficient individual activity and participation by the children, the teacher will now wish to look for something which rounds off this work and allows the children to see or experience the work they have done in a wider context: perhaps another *bear* story or some jingles with *b* words, or the compilation of a wall chart containing illustrations connected with a story which contains several *b* words. These could be labelled and the *b* sound emphasised.
- To round off the lesson the children's attention must be brought back to the specific purpose of the work: to recognise the letter *b* by name and by sound within the context of a word beginning with *b*. These two things must be left clearly in their minds. For this purpose, the reflective period should not be cluttered or confusing.

Introducing words: the beginnings of word recognition

Introduction to words should proceed through a developing progression, generally speaking from the known to the unknown, from the familiar to the unfamiliar, from words of simple structure to those that are more complex. Continuously call attention to common words in the first place and show children the printed form that can be associated with the spoken word or object. For example, show them the lavatories with the associated labels *boys* and *girls*. Follow this up with clothes pegs showing each child's name, and then with labels on things in the classroom – window, wall, door, floor, table, desk. Do not expect children at first to analyse the words, but stress corresponding sounds – /w/ at the beginning of your pronunciation of *window* and *wall* – and point in passing to the corresponding parts of words such as *door, floor, chair, chalk*. Eventually expect children to point to these correspondences of letters and to draw attention to corresponding sounds.

Show children words that match objects, especially intimate objects such as toys and possessions, for example: *teddy, ball*, or *cap*; and add to them: *bounce the ball, hug teddy, red cap, my cap*, and make up little statements around them. Use word cards, but remember that it is essential for children to witness how you write words for them. Try not to present previously written word cards as a fait accompli. Let children witness the formulation of letters and the construction of words as you write them.

Introduction to word study

Teach children to look at words, to compare words and to look for differences and similarities:

Jane's coat, David's coat;
door, floor; toy, boy;
bat, but; cap, cat.

Onomatopoeia has great appeal to children and is an excellent device for emphasising sound: *splash, swish, plunge, bang, plod, prod.*

Similarly, nursery rhymes emphasise sound correspondences: *peep, sheep; Horner, corner; Jill* and *hill.*

It is important to remember that it is futile merely to ask children to look at words and phrases; they must be trained to look at them for specific purposes. This can be done in various ways, the main ones being:

1 when asking children to look at words in the hope that they will draw comparisons, teachers should rewrite the words in the presence of the children, pronouncing the words emphatically and using colour or underlining to emphasise the similarities or differences. At first this should be done in passing, but gradually teachers will expect some evidence of memorising taking place;

2 using wooden cut-out letters, children should be encouraged to match the words. This illustrates and emphasises order, sequence and orientation of the individual letters. Children can easily place a wooden letter upside down or the wrong way round or in the wrong position in the word, which provides the teacher with the opportunity to rectify this and thereby emphasise orientation, order and position of the letters in a word;

3 children with growing experience could be expected to make selections from an array, such as, *sleep* from *Peep, sheep, sleep.* It is the ability to make fine distinctions that is crucial in learning to read; little skill is needed to distinguish between *cat* and *aeroplane*, although initially such crude distinctions will need to be practised. Furthermore, this is an important step towards identifying and distinguishing between the parts of a syllable known as onset and rime (see Adams, 1992, p. 308).

Letter formation

Get children to trace with their forefinger, overwrite or copy familiar words. Show them how to form letters, where to start – b at the top of the down stroke, d at the higher point where the circle leaves the ascender – and what sequence to follow – b down the ascender then up and clockwise, d anticlockwise, up the ascender and down again. Each letter should be similarly formed each time it is written, because the way in which letters are formed determines the ease with which children can adapt to cursive or joined up writing as it is called. Undoubtedly it is easier for the beginner to form the letters f, k, s, x and z in their printed form. However, steps must be taken at a reasonably early stage to teach children the cursive form of these letters:

f k s x y

Again with these cursive forms, the starting point and the sequence or track of the pencil are crucial if somewhat obvious. (For an alternative approach to letter formation see Chapter 7.) Remember to teach children how to hold a pencil and how to sit when writing, and keep on reminding them of these throughout the infant classes. Children should be taught to sit squarely at a desk, place the paper at a slight angle towards the left if the writer is right-handed and towards the right if the writer is left-handed. The pencil or pen should lie easily between the forefinger and thumb and rest lightly upon the second finger. The grip should be light and the forefinger held in a relaxed curve, not in an inverted v, desperately gripping manner. To write in this way requires a soft pencil and an easy flowing roller ball or fountain pen. The normal ballpoint (Bic etc.) is not an appropriate instrument: the flow of ink is not sufficient to allow a very light touch, and bad habits ensue from having to put undue pressure on the pen whilst writing. Tracing with the forefinger comes first as it is the easiest of the writing tasks, whilst overwriting can raise anxiety if children are expected to be over-meticulous in following the original precisely.

Introduction to words in a text

| It's | my | birthday | today | . | I | am | seven | . |

Look at the words with the children; note *birthday* and *today* and comment upon the similarities. Note *seven* and suggest that it starts like *six*.

If your school has the *Breakthrough to Literacy Teacher's Sentence Maker* and *Word Bank* so much the better. Use it as a group exercise. It makes a wonderful introduction to the composition of continuous prose; a child makes a statement and the teacher selects and arranges the words in the trough. Then teacher and children read the text together. Similarly, the nursery rhymes and known jingles can be reconstructed with the relevant word cards produced by the teacher.

When using the technique of labelling, take advantage of the opportunity to introduce structure words that do not usually stand alone:

the door
a jar of sugar
here are the paints
there is water in the tap
this is the cold water tap.

This illustrates the nature of text and it shows how texts can be built up.

All the suggestions so far involve the children actively in the study of words, which can be regarded as the beginnings of instruction in spelling and handwriting, as well as in word recognition.

Story telling, composing a text and reading

Gradually, shared story composition will emerge, with a teacher and a group of children working together to compose a text. In an example where the teacher wrote the label, *the paints*, the following text emerged through discussion. It was written down by the teacher acting as prompter and scribe:

We mix the paints,
then we draw on the paper.
We used a lot of colours.

The children 'read' and 'reread' it many times from memory. Note the change of tense. This occurred as a result of the questions posed by the teacher and showed a keen response by five- to six-year-olds to the language used by the teacher. It illuminates the need for great care in language usage by teachers.

For a different perspective, train children in the reception class to operate a tape recorder, so that they can tell stories or record orally events of the day or previous evening. These recordings can be transcribed and subsequently read aloud to the children with encouragement for them to read along with the teacher. This is another way of showing children how texts are made by involving them in the process.

Story telling by the children, whether transcribed subsequently by the teacher or by the child, should play a continuing part in the process of learning to read and write.

No opportunity should be missed to stimulate story telling, both individually and as a group. Get children to bring toys, photographs and illustrations to school and encourage them to talk about them, describe them and romanticise about them. This is the beginning of the composition of texts. It stimulates thought and expands the children's universe; it helps them to break out of their immediate environment; and it provides them with a background for new experiences in thought, imagery, language and action.

Children love to hear stories, especially stories about other children who perform deeds that they would like to perform but hardly dare do so. Therefore, it will be very rewarding to the teacher and the children if he or she creates a pair or small gang of children who operate in an environment identifiable to the children. From this the teacher can develop spontaneous short stories of a few minutes' duration, each an episode in the doings of the chosen pair or gang. This would present the class with a chain of thought, so that periodically they can compose episodes themselves. They have a framework within which their minds can create ideas, images and sequences. This will help to develop the skill of composing that will eventually underpin their ability to produce written language.

Constrained composition and reading

By way of contrast to the expansive story telling referred to in the previous section, periodically employ a more severely controlled form of composing and link it closely with the act of reading. Write single-sentence stories for children and then read them together in order to foster a 'feeling' for reading. Then get children to try to write the sentence, copying it however inaccurately. Play a game of trying to write 'My own sentence'. Afterwards write the correct version underneath – not as correction, but merely as 'I would write it like this . . .' Let them copy what you have written and note how their letter formations are progressing. Give further instructions on letter formation and general tips on writing words, but on a separate occasion.

When writing for children, always use capital letters where appropriate and correct punctuation, and encourage them from the beginning to try to emulate you, especially in using capitals at the beginning and full stops at the ends of sentences. It is surprising how much children learn incidentally through observation of adult behaviour.

Blending

Soon after children have begun to recognise a few common words and have developed a familiarity with letters, you should begin to point to blends as in: *brown bread; brown bread and brown eggs for breakfast.*

Use colour to highlight the blends and always give further examples in order to reinforce what the children see. For example:

playing . . . *pl*aying *at* *pl*aytime *in the* *pl*ayground with *pl* highlighted,

*kit**ch**en* . . . Mummy was stit*ch*ing *in the kit**ch**en, with* *ch* highlighted and

*gn**ome** . . . **gn**at, **gn**aw, **gn**ome*, with *gn* highlighted.

Remember always to ensure that the meaning of the word is understood and that graphemic and phonological elements are always presented within a meaningful unit, that is within a word, a phrase or a sentence. Phonics is meaningless out of context, but it can be used, and even understood, by children if they encounter it as part of familiar words. An over-emphasis on sound to the exclusion of meaning can pose problems, as in the case where a child gets as far as the /pi:/ sound in *people* but does not recognise the sound of the other letters combined. If, however, children are being trained to look for meaning as well as sound, then with developing flexibility and thought there is a chance of successful guessing. This is another instance where training in the adoption of searching behaviour is crucial. If children are expected to make sense in their responses, they will search for sense; if not, they will be content to utter the first thing that comes into their mind, which may or may not make sense.

Nursery rhymes and 'pretend' reading

Play 'pretend reading', using nursery rhymes, with a group of children reading from the overhead projector:

Jack and Jill went up the . . . (teacher writes in the missing word)

To fetch a pail of . . . (again the teacher writes in the missing word so that the children witness word construction).

This activity builds confidence, familiarity with words and a disposition to predict using text that has been read. It also provides opportunities for the teacher to point out words and draw comparisons with other words – words of similar construction or with words that have common features.

Some children will be able to join in this activity more knowingly than others. Those who appear hesitant can be taken aside, either individually or in pairs, and, using a book or printed sheet this time, you can follow similar but more pointed procedures. It will allow you to indicate more clearly to the children what you are doing and the type of behaviour you expect of them. For example, you will be able to indicate clearly that it is not merely a matter of repeating by heart the nursery rhyme in your case; you are also following the printed text and matching what you say to specific places in the text: namely, that you are proceeding from left to right and, at this stage, word by word from top to bottom.

Occasionally, possibly with some frequency, one or more of the children will make incorrect responses. This you can take as your mistake and in self-correcting the mistake yourself you will begin to convey to the children the need to pay close attention to the text. It will be also a tentative beginning of self-correcting behaviour, one of the behavioural skills in reading emphasised by Clay (1993).

This idea of 'pretend' reading with the teacher is such an important activity in preparing children for learning to read that it should be repeated many times during the preparatory period. Apart from anything else it gives children who have little experience of books in the home a clear idea of a general approach to reading, without of course the details of word identification. Children can witness superficially what you are doing and can try to emulate you.

In order to emphasise the importance of 'reading' with the teacher as an activity that should receive serious attention, the following procedures are suggested as a basis for placing the activities within the literacy hour as suggested in the National Literacy Strategy document (1997):

1 Begin by telling the class what they are going to do and give them a synopsis of the nursery rhyme in order to remind them of its contents, to stimulate interest and to set their minds working on the contextual meaning of the chosen nursery rhyme.

2 With the class facing the overhead projector you read aloud the nursery rhyme with the children accompanying you, pretending to read. After praising their efforts, repeat the process. Highlight a common word here and there in the text; the number of times chosen will depend upon the children's experience. At the same time children will each have a card

containing the word. You can point to features of the word, for example, its initial letter or its length, to make the children direct their attention to the word. Then during a further reading from the OHP the children are required to hold up the word card when that word is encountered in the reading by you and the children.

3 Children are divided into groups according to the quality of their contributions in the above class activity. All will have copies of the nursery rhyme printed with double or treble spaces between the lines and reasonable spaces between the words. The least able children will have to match the one word card to the corresponding words in the nursery rhyme; others will have additional word cards to match, underlining them in the rhyme; more advanced children can attempt to overwrite or even copy the words under the corresponding words in the text.

Whilst these activities are proceeding you will have an opportunity to go through the reading together activity with the more hesitant children, giving them extra support and encouragement.

Other activities with the selected common words can involve finger tracing and looking for those words in other texts selected by you beforehand as containing those words.

4 Returning the whole class to the OHP, this time using a copy of the nursery rhyme with the common words omitted, you read aloud accompanied by the children who try to insert orally the missing words. These are immediately written onto the OHP by you, allowing the children to watch your careful formulation of the letters of the word. Don't at this stage expect the children to give you the letters unless they do so voluntarily. However, if they do offer the letters they should be congratulated, so that they begin to realise that there is more to reading than mere 'magic' by the teacher.

5 In a final reflective activity ask the children to mention any words, or even phrases, that they remember from the nursery rhyme. As these are given they can be written on the OHP or the blackboard and commented upon by you. For example, you could stress the initial sound (they will have been working on the alphabet and its sounds in previous lessons) or, if given a phrase, you could illustrate its composition containing several words. This could then be rounded off with a final teacher and class reading of the complete text.

There can be many variations of these suggestions provided that the objectives are kept clearly in mind. These are that growing confidence is fostered and that children get a sense of the general behaviour required of readers without, at this stage, the burden of close word analysis and identification, even though in other aspects of the literacy development programme they will be experiencing some initial forms of word analysis, as in the previous section on blending.

Exploratory writing

Do not miss any opportunities to encourage children to try as early as possible to write for themselves. Although you will be giving instruction, lasting a few moments every day, in the formation of letters, do not discourage imaginative attempts and, if they have 'written a story' for you, accept it seriously and, as part of your response, write a correct version underneath. Children will emulate your writing, so correctness of form on your part is essential.

Point out the punctuation you use as you write, not after you have written, otherwise punctuation will be taken as an after thought, whereas you want to impress upon them that punctuation is part and parcel of writing.

Exploratory 'pretend' writing is an important cognitive exercise in which children try to use what they know or perceive about writing in order to express their thoughts. It is an important staging post en route for composing and writing texts.

However, at this stage children will be experiencing two impulses. One is to express themselves in written form copying what they think adults are engaged in: namely, putting pencil or pen marks on paper which represent a message or story. The other impulse is a growing realisation that those marks represent in some specific way what the adults say. In other words, they realise that sound and writing somehow coincide. They have been introduced to the alphabet and are some way into learning that letters correspond to sounds and this triggers a desire to try and link the two together. Furthermore, they have experience of print in some sort of vague way in their environment as Gibson and Levin (1975) show and, consequently, they are beginning to be aware that letters, in addition to standing in isolation, also stand in groups. To this notion adults attach the term *word*.

Hence, there arises an ideal opportunity for teachers to encourage children in their exploratory writing to bring some kind of order to their scribbles by inventing the traces of spelling which can be formulated as time passes into a spelling system through additional teaching and guidance.

The following is offered as a rough guide in planning a lesson for 5- or 6-year-old children which incorporates exploratory writing and inventive spelling within the context of stories and reading:

1 Begin with an introduction to the whole class using the nursery rhyme, *Pussycat, pussycat, where have you been?* Have enlarged pictures of cats with enlarged writing showing the words *pussycat* underneath each picture. These should be held forward for the children to see as the words are repeated in the nursery rhyme.

2 This can be followed by a discussion about the story and its cat. The children should be encouraged to speak and express any ideas they may have about cats.

3 Then write slowly the word *pussycat* on the blackboard and pronounce each segment of the words as you do so. Repeat this, encouraging the children to join in the pronunciation of the word so that the process of linking letters to the sounds is established, or re-established as the case may be. As you do this, emphasise what you are doing by saying repeatedly to the children, 'As I say the words I am going to write them'.

4 Next, the children working independently draw a picture of a cat engaged in some activity such as sitting under a chair or climbing a tree. When they have finished the drawing they are told to write underneath the drawing what the pussycat is doing. The term *pussycat* as opposed to *cat* alone is used partly because of its place in the nursery rhyme but partly also because it is a more intimate term for the animal, and therefore more attractive to young children. As this individual activity proceeds you can circulate, commenting upon the attempts of the children, especially their attempts to write and spell, which are the main purpose of the exercise. Call the children's attention to one another's efforts and in as many cases as possible recite what the children have 'written' underneath their efforts so that they can draw their own comparisons without experiencing any criticism from you.

5 Following this individual activity by the children you can draw them together round the blackboard and, asking individual children to 'read' out their story, transpose the story onto the blackboard and invite all to join you in 'reading' the story aloud.

6 The children's interest and involvement should be intense at this point, so to capitalise on their keenness, they can be asked either to try to copy the story from the board or to write any other story they might have thought of as a result of hearing other children's stories. Again you would circulate and comment constructively. This is not a test of what the children can do but an opportunity for them to experiment.

As part of this development, you will begin to write two-sentence stories for the children, centred upon some toy, object or event that has just happened. A child dictates: *Jenny was playing with the water tray. William pushed it over.*

There are opportunities here to refer to capital letters used to begin sentences and children's names, and to point to the use of full stops. The same sentences can be used to illustrate the use of the comma by joining the two sentences with a conjunction: *Jenny was playing with the water tray, so William pushed it over.*

Again a reference to capital letters can be made showing that William starts with a capital W, because William is a boy's name and names begin with a capital letter, and add, 'Just as your name begins with a capital . . .'

It is continuous and frequent references of this nature that gradually begin to penetrate the children's view of writing and their understanding of the nature of text.

And and *then* are the conjunctions children use in the early stages, but soon they must encounter a greater range of conjunctions – *if, so, but, because, when*. It is by using these words that they can introduce reasoning into their texts. Two-sentence statements are an ideal vehicle.

> *Jenny wanted to play with the water tray, but William pushed it over.*
> *We came in from play. It was raining.* Why did we come in from play?
> *We came in from play, because it was raining.*

This problem can be dealt with in this rather formal way only by working with the children in a 'workshop approach', whereby two-sentence statements are examined, their meaning discussed and consideration given to a possible solution. For example, the use of *but* in the example above must be seen as introducing a qualifying element, whereas *because* is a means of explaining an action. The connections that these two words bring about must be clearly understood. Other examples must be considered which have been specially designed by the teacher to elucidate the effect of using these particular words.

In addition to this rather formal approach, it is important to follow it up by taking every opportunity to demonstrate how these connectives can be used correctly by amending what the children have written. Do not hesitate to use one child's words to demonstrate to the class the effect this practice of amending has upon the way in which ideas are expressed. Only by continual reminders and over a considerable number of years will the children become practised in the use of connectives.

Although children may be slow to grasp the use of connectives in their written work they will be able to cope much earlier in the spoken medium. This suggests that an important place should

be reserved for oral practice in developing children's understanding of and development in language.

Preparing to read the first book

Take words from the proposed first reading book and use them
as in the previous four sections above. Play games of 'I know that
word', 'I can trace with my finger that word', 'I can copy that word'
and even, 'I can write that word' (emergent writing). Even if the
child 'makes a hash' of writing the word, treat the act of trying
approvingly, but write your version underneath.

Introducing the first book

Tell the children what it is about, whet their appetites, make them
think *you* want to read the book. Reintroduce some, if not all, of
the words that will appear in the first reading book on cards and
place them alongside the characters and objects that make up the
contents of the book. Encourage the children to memorise these
words and phrases, so that they will recognise them when they
encounter them in their first book. The timing of this introduction
will depend upon several things: pre-school experiences with
books and print, intelligence, aptitude and the emphases of the
work in the reception class. This introductory process should be
regarded as a distinct step or series of steps leading up to and
preparatory to the first actual reading. It should not be regarded
as a short and immediate preamble to the reading.

Reading their first books

1 You read to the child – the child tries to read with you.
2 The characters and objects are introduced separately with their
  accompanying words and phrases – talk about them, write out
  the words in the presence of the child and get the child to try
  to recognise them.
3 Encourage the child to try to read with your prompting and
  treat a child's attempts to read a book as a learning experience
  and not an occasion for testing ability.

Listening to children read

Whenever a child is reading aloud always have a notepad by you.
Write down for the child any word that causes difficulty.
Demonstrate how you would read it, emphasising the segments
or syllables or letter strings: /br/, /ed/; /bre/, /d/; /str/, /iŋ/; /stri/,
/ŋ/.

Finally, pronounce them normally as /striŋ/ (string), /bred/ (bread), thus indicating that the child has to look for units within words. /k//æ//t/ is manageable, but the word represented by the letters s, l, i, g, h, t, l, y is confusing, so *sl, ight, ly* is the only option and the child must seek out the appropriate clusters as well as devising a means of blending the elements together.

Encourage children to think about **what** and **how** they read. Judge when it is feasible to begin using the modified miscue analysis, suggested in *Miscue analysis and listening to children read* on page 49. It establishes a workshop approach to listening to children read and gets away from the passive 'barking at print'.

Word recognition: contrastive discrimination

Also on your notepad, when you write a word that is causing difficulty try to write and pronounce another word with a contrasting feature:

sing, song, singing;
light, fight;
string, strong string.

Do not worry about exactness so long as you call attention to the words. The idea is to get children to discriminate between words. Get the child to think of rhyming words – refer to nursery rhymes whenever possible, for example: *sheep: Little Bo Peep has lost her . . .* (allow the child to predict the last word).

Look for rhyming words, such as *fly, sky; coat, boat; light, might*; mix up print and illustrations and pictures and get children to match them up.

Play spontaneous I-spy games, dealing only with a few words at a time. There are ample opportunities in these activities for oral experimentation and teacher–child discussion.

Whenever possible or appropriate set these words in a context so that their meaning and their usage is clear. For example, if the child stumbles over the word *thought* the first thing is to establish its derivation by giving the contrasting statements:

I thought I saw you this morning.
I think I shall see you tomorrow morning.

These two sentences are spoken by the teacher. The next thing is to draw comparisons which will help to impress the spelling of the word upon the child's memory. The word *thought* is written with the words *bought* and *fought* written alongside. Comparisons of the spelling are drawn orally and highlighting or underlining is used for emphasis. It is important to combine a visual and an oral input and to couch the words in a meaningful context.

Developing word recognition skills

Alongside the second, third and fourth reading book stage, it is important to implement a more rigorous programme for developing word recognition skills. Knowing a number of familiar common words, the individual letters of the alphabet and the initial and final two-letter blends, will not get the children very far. However, along with their experience of print, they will have been imbibing a hazy familiarity with English spelling patterns. Now their awareness of letter-strings, syllables and spelling patterns should be heightened so that these become more overtly recognised. Word families emphasise similarities between the members, but also they illustrate word structure and prepare children for the syllabic nature of words: *sing, sling, sting, string, spring, bring, cling, wing.*

These words can be divided into onset and rime, the latter being the vowel plus consonant or consonant string: *s - ing; spr - ing.*

In a similar way the consonant digraphs – *ch, sh, th* (the two forms), *ph, kn, ght, wr, ck*; the silent letters as in *gnat* and *gnome, lamb* and *limb, know* and *knew, psalm* and *psychic, island* and *isle*; and the tenses of verbs – regular at first with *ed* for the past tense and subsequently the irregular forms such as *grow, growing, grew,* and *go, going, went,* can be introduced as word families.

Now it is not merely a matter of posting up charts of word families, and it is not a matter of rote learning in the form of drill. All these features of words will appear as the children proceed through the reading schemes – whether published scheme or 'real books' – and as schemes vary it is up to teachers to write a programme of word recognition study that dovetails into the progression of the scheme. Even the most comprehensive schemes published cannot provide the necessary instructions nor adequately practise the children in all these elements. Thus, teachers and their notepads are crucial factors in any reading scheme.

And there is one further point that was made in an earlier chapter, and that is that concentrating upon the rime elements in words is an excellent form of recognition and comparison between words, but it has its limitations in practising the blending of syllables. Therefore, it is important also to emphasise continually an alternative way of pronouncing words in order to set up a habit of blending the onset with the vowel, for example, /stri/, /ŋ/, is said, having recognised the visual image as *str-ing.*

When using word cards for display or for quick recognition exercises, they could be bent at the boundaries between the onset and the rime to encourage awareness of the clustering of letters (*fl-ight*), but a duplicate copy, in another colour ink, could be bent to illustrate easy blending (*fli-ght*).

Polysyllabic words will have to be dealt with in a very clear and methodical way. The syllables will have to be indicated by emphasis in speech but this is merely as a guide to children. They themselves will have to acquire a disposition of looking for and identifying the syllables of a word. Here both teaching and experience are necessary, so bent word cards and colour highlighting by the teacher will help to instil the syllabic patterns of polysyllabic words. Build up from morphemes – pen/cil, lamp/light, pass/word. Encourage finger tracing whilst saying the morphemes or syllables, to be followed by writing the word without copying, which encourages conscious retention.

All the activities connected with the development of word recognition skills should involve finger tracing, vocalisation, and writing, at least until the child has learned how to learn words. Writing the words without copying acts as a check upon whether the word has been learned and it adds to the kinaesthetic sense in learning the word and impressing it upon the memory of the learner.

Additionally, children should always have the words placed in context for them and they should then attempt to place those words in a textual setting by composing a written message that contains them.

Remember to build into your programme opportunities for plenty of recall and reinforcement. Letters, words, phrases are rarely learnt on one occasion. Half a dozen repetitions is too few for some things to be learned.

During the earlier stages of learning to read, do not require children to pick up a book and read it to you unpractised. Get them to read it over silently first so that they will begin to formulate their ideas about the content of the text. Encourage them to note words that they cannot recognise, so that you can tell them what the words are before they begin reading aloud to you. You may even prefer to teach them something about the words they do not recognise, such as helping them to search for pronounceable parts and drawing comparisons with similarities in other known words. At other times you will wish to leave this teaching until after the passage has been read to you. What is certain, however, is that such teaching is absolutely essential at some point. Reading aloud to the teacher should be regarded as a workshop-like activity, not as a test of performance.

Reading in meaningful segments

As children progress on to third, fourth and fifth books, try to get them to read in pairs of words and then in phrases thus: *We / shall / play / with / the / ball*; reread, *We shall / play / with the ball*; and, as progress is made: *We shall play / with the ball*.

Thus you will create a disposition to look for groups of words rather than dwell upon single words when reading.

Reading what they have written previously helps greatly, because they are fully conversant with how they want to express something. Always encourage rhythmic reading with variations in pace, tone and pitch. Expression not only helps listeners, it helps readers to process meaning more effectively because the search for expression entails a search for meaning (Perera, 1989).

Incidentally, it has been known for teachers to tell children when reading aloud to 'put expression into it'. However, telling in this way is not particularly helpful. You should not only read with expression when reading aloud to the children, you should demonstrate how you do it, calling attention to the demands of the text and the ways of meeting those demands. Many children will find this difficult and they will require specific and determined teaching as well as subsequent reminders. Marked texts which have oblique strokes marking the phrases will help greatly.

This training has an additional purpose; it will begin to influence the ways in which the children read silently provided the teacher encourages the children to consciously try to identify phrases when reading silently. Skill in doing this will only develop if reminders are given and if marked passages, highlighted in colour, are provided. Skilled reading of this nature is not something that is easily achieved, and in any case it will not develop to any significant degree until the later stages of the primary school. Nevertheless, the foundations can be laid much earlier.

Textual understanding

Develop this growing ability to manipulate a text through sequencing exercises:

1 cut up nursery rhymes into verses first, then into lines, and reassemble;
2 cut up two-sentence stories and reassemble;
3 cut up simple stories and reassemble.

The way in which these nursery rhymes, two-sentence stories and simple prose are cut up should vary according to the ability of the children as should the activities that are involved in the exercise. In the first place it will be teacher and child working together to reassemble the basic elements of the text. For example, the lines of a nursery rhyme or the two sections in a two-sentence story. Later it will involve the verses of a nursery rhyme or the sentences of a short story with decisions to be made concerning their proper sequence. Ambiguity will lead to greater intensity of thought being required to resolve the sequence.

These activities can be carried out individually, in pairs and in groups with the teacher periodically participating in order to provide guidance by example.

Later, in the junior school, employ more complex texts, so that more detailed thought has to be given to their resolution. Do it as a teacher-led group exercise first, then individually or as a peer group exercise. Remember, here is an ideal opportunity for oral discussion about sequence and hence about meaning.

Each teacher should endeavour to build up an adequate classified store of sequencing materials which can be accessed easily for specific teaching purposes or by the children for practice in the exercise of meaning and the construction of texts.

Cloze procedure and comprehension

Again on a teacher-led group basis first, and afterwards as peer group discussions and individual exercises, play 'Guess the missing word(s); – prepare short cloze passages such as: *In the play . . . we kick the . . .*

Sometimes omit every nth word, sometimes particular parts of speech or phrases. Discussion is an important part of the exercise, and especially discussion of ambiguities. The use of software – *TRAY* for example – can be effective.

The following is a possible sequence for a literacy hour period dealing with a specific problem, in this case the use of adverbs ending with the suffix *ly*:

1 Teacher raises the problem and poses the question of correct or incorrect use by giving two sentences, one of which is incorrect.

   The boy was running quick.
   The boy was running quickly.

   Class discuss with teacher and offer similar instances with the teacher responding and commenting. These offerings are written up on the blackboard or OHP (i.e. the correct versions only for positive reinforcement purposes).
2 Teacher displays on the OHP a short text with the adverb(s) missing. The class respond and the teacher comments.
3 Individuals have a cloze exercise with the adverbs missing or written incorrectly (i.e. without the suffix *ly*).

4 Teacher goes through this exercise on the OHP with the class. The pupils check their efforts. Points can be raised and problems resolved by teacher–child discussion in front of the class so that all hear.

5 Individually the children compose and write a short text containing four or five adverbs ending in *ly*.

6 Teacher selects children to read their efforts to the class and each contribution is discussed.

Other forms of adverb and adverbial phrase will be dealt with in a slightly different manner. This is because their positional use is not so apparent and a greater degree of explanation will be necessary, especially with the less able children or children with limited experience of spoken and written language. This demands closer work with particular children which means small group or individual instruction with specific and precise guidance given. Consequently, the above sequence of activities would need a slight alteration to item 3. Instead of this stage in the lesson being regarded as a test or practice session concerned with what has been learned without too much difficulty by children in the upper primary school, there will be a need for further teaching and closer guidance in working out the identification of and, more importantly, the position of adverbs such as *just*, *only*, *soon*, *somehow*, *therefore*, and *whereby*. Hence, there is a need to work with small groups at this stage of the lesson to ensure through close observation of each child's reactions to your explanations that they have been fully understood. Clear guidance for teachers can be found in Crystal (1992) pages 150–5.

From this variation in classroom organisation it can be seen that the subject matter of the lesson can and frequently does define the type of organisation that is necessary. Small group work is sometimes crucial whilst at other times some aspects of literacy can be explained easily and practised with the whole class as a single unit. Some parts of the literacy programme are straightforward, requiring little explanation and are easily understood, whilst other parts are ambiguous, requiring detailed explanations and, even then, need further reflection in order to incorporate them fully into normal usage. An example of the latter – dealing with ability to use semantic and syntactic cues – follows:

1 General talk to class about using and working on a text, involving prediction, inductive thinking, forward and backward cuing.

2 Class trial with a short passage with cloze omissions on the OHP. Oral responses from the class and teacher reactions.

3 Several cloze passages adjusted to the abilities of three or more groups. Each group in discussion attempts to resolve the

omissions, the teacher circulating and participating in these discussions. These passages can range from the straightforward to the ambiguous. The latter will be designed to provoke discussion and argument within the group, and the answer may depend upon close reasoning or even personal preference.

e.g.   High winds are *frightening*.
or   High winds are *invigorating*.

The answer may depend upon some cue in the text or it may depend upon the feelings of the reader. In either case, the choice of word has to be justified.

4 Next there follows a search on an individual basis in literature or prepared texts for examples of instances where an alternative word could be substituted, either to retain or to change the meaning of the sentence.

5 Coming together again as a class, instances are read out by individual children. These are given some consideration by other children and by the teacher, with the teacher using these examples to remind children of the need to reflect upon the overall meaning of a text as well as on the meaning of separated component parts of that text.

These examples are given in order to illustrate the possibility of adjusting the organisation of teaching to suit the requirements of the subject matter and the varying needs of children. Organisation of lessons, like the arrangement of classroom furniture, should not be static.

Cloze procedure, then, is a useful vehicle for individual, small group and class work. Through it many facts can be learned with minimum teacher input to a full class and with frequent practice.

However, it is through group, including teacher, interaction that children learn to use their experiences as well semantic and syntactic cues to help them resolve phono-graphemic difficulties presented by unfamiliar words.

Further developments in the junior school

Remember that between six and nine years of age is a crucial time in children's reading development. The majority have a fair amount of skill, but it is not yet a complete automatic skill and they are beginning to come face to face with many more new words as they explore the world of books. Therefore two things are necessary. Make time and provision for the children to choose books that take their fancy. Encourage them to read silently, to discover what they like and to express this orally and in writing. Do not accept puerile book reviews; accept only genuine reactions to and thoughts about books. Make it a challenge to write something important about the books they have just read, because you and other children will be interested in their reactions to a book. Periodically set three or more children to read the same book, simultaneously if possible, and then join with them in discussing the book: the plot, the characters, the children's reactions to events. Encourage them to note, collect and remember any new words that they encounter. Secondly, set time limits for reading a popular easy-to-read book or series so that children are in fact racing against time and one another to complete the book or books. This 'jerks' them out of a lethargic way of reading. Some teachers suggest books and encourage this type of reading for the holidays.

Eventually, at the top of the junior school you will be able to probe more deeply into such matters as the bias or sympathy of the author, the morality expressed within the book and the language of the text. Research by the Family Reading Groups Project (UKRA) has pointed to the advantages of getting parents to join discussions of books; the project officers suggest that discussions, in which parents, children and the teacher are equal participants, lead to increased discrimination among all readers including those who are at the hesitant stage.

With growing competence in the outwardly visible manifestations of reading, it will be necessary to teach children how to comprehend a text. Now it is known that readers build up the message of a text from the words, from their particular arrangement (syntax) and from an interpretation of these in the light of the reader's experience and from extra contextual cues. Skilled readers accomplish this as they process the text, but children must be helped to develop a disposition to process what they read. They cannot be relied upon to develop this facility naturally, especially if they are allowed to over-indulge in reading slowly word by word. Furthermore, they may read so few things that really grip their imagination sufficiently to make them want to remember exactly what they have read. One of the benefits of mathematics books, in which the problems are posed in language terms, is that they ensure that the children have to remember what they have read in order to solve the problems. Thus when reading to the teacher, children in the middle stages of learning to read should be urged to read more quickly and in meaningful phrases, and they should be stopped at various junctures in the text and asked to recall what they have read up to that point. Similarly, they should be aware that at the end of the reading they may be required to retell their story in their own words. This ensures a commitment to try to remember the message and it is an invaluable mental activity in the processing of information. It is also a superb exercise in oral composing – knowledge telling as it has been designated by Bereiter and Scardamalia (1987) – and contributes significantly to the development of children's writing ability.

Perera (1984) shows that many difficulties in reading have their source in the grammatical structure of texts. She argues that reading is likely to be harder 'when the grammatical structure of a sentence is not easy to predict'; concealed negatives as in 'The fox is rarely seen in town', or inverted word order, such as 'Without speaking he left the room' could cause difficulty for the unskilled reader. Similarly, over-long phrases and unwieldy clausal structures make sentences less manageable, as does a sentence that has too many bits of information which the reader cannot readily and easily chunk together to form a more complete and hence a more memorable statement. This applies equally to a passage 'when a heavy burden is imposed on short-term memory' with too many unco-ordinated facts to be retained in order to understand the full text. These are problems which are not easily dealt with by young readers, even those who appear to read well in the upper stages of the primary school. For this reason Perera suggests that it would be unwise to present children solely with texts that are uncomplicated, with a message that unfolds logically and predictably and which contain reasonably short clauses and sentences. They should experience, in Perera's view, texts which do present difficulties for the reader and to this end she makes a number of important suggestions for practising teachers. First, the teacher should continue, throughout the infant school years and beyond into the junior school years, to read aloud to the class, choosing texts containing 'the more literary discourse structures and sentence patterns'. She goes on to suggest the selection of texts upon which teacher and children can work together in order to learn more about their structure. The activities include marking on the text the connectives, the cohesive ties which connect persons and things within the text, the demarcation of noun and verb phrases, the identification of interrupting constructions and the noting of the attendant punctuation marks. She also suggests devices for inserting these structural markers into a text. These include rearranging jumbled sentences using the connectives as a guide, and filling in gaps, perhaps from a multiple-choice list, where connectives have been omitted. These latter activities fall into the same constructive approach to texts as does composition and writing.

Naturally, the selection of texts will need careful consideration. Perera (1984) gives many examples in order to illustrate her argument. From these primary school teachers will be able to construct their own texts upon which they and the children can work. This leads to another point: one which profoundly affects children's understanding.

It would seem futile to regard work on these texts as an individual activity to be set without prior discussion and considerable teaching on every occasion. Discussion can take place on a class basis with the teacher demonstrating on the overhead projector with members of the class being asked to participate in ways other than as mere observers. This can be followed by the class working on the texts in pairs and being encouraged to discuss what is being done. This form of organisation has the advantage over individuals working discretely in that the points at issue are emphasised and illuminated in the process of co-operative activity. A child working alone gets it right or wrong, whereas a child working with another has to argue his or her case.

However, this is not the end of the process. Work on such difficult things as grammatical structure will require, in many cases, further intensive instruction, which will be most effectively carried out by the teacher working with small groups of children, demonstrating and guiding the children by using further examples and requiring the children to demonstrate their new-found ability. In this way the new knowledge will be generalised and incorporated into practical usage. After this has been accomplished practice exercises can be set for individual work.

In the above sequence of classroom activities there is sufficient variety to fulfil the requirements of the literacy hour.

Composing as a basis for more advanced reading development

Much of the writing that is done between the ages of six and ten will be based upon events that the children have witnessed, stories that they have heard, journeys that they have made, and activities in which they have participated. The basis of this writing is repetition and regurgitation. The children's task is to recall what they know and transcribe it into a text, preferably for a stated specific audience. The inexperienced teacher needs to realise that these transcriptions will vary greatly in length. Some will consist of a single sentence whilst others will amount to a page or more of writing. It is important that this should be so, because children must learn that the length of a text depends upon its purpose. If the purpose is simply to state the colour of a friend's eyes then a short sentence is all that is necessary, whereas the description of an involved and complex journey requires a lengthier text. All too often children are unsure of how much they should write. The answer is, of course, 'as much as is necessary', and it is at this point that teacher–child discussion about the purpose of the writing will guide the inexperienced writer.

The important basis of this 'knowledge-telling' type of writing is that the children have something to tell. Listening to a piece of music, looking at a picture, or handling a piece of driftwood does not necessarily inspire a flow of well-formed prose. In fact such activities can be a source of confusion, unless teachers suggest ideas and stimulate, provoke and guide the thoughts of the children. Children need to have ideas 'fed into them' just as actors and actresses need a good producer to direct their thoughts and actions. It is insufficient to give only an initial stimulus. It is part of the teacher's task to maintain a high level of motivation throughout the writing process.

An initial stimulus is, of course, necessary but there is also a need to introduce stimuli and guidance at all stages. For example, following the initial stimulus the children will need help in formulating thoughts prior to writing and they will need to be guided in their choice of words and phrases central to the message. Then as they write and inevitably run out of ideas, a response by the teacher to what they have written up to that point may trigger further thought. Alternatively it may be necessary for the teacher to suggest something (Figure 3.2).

Finally, the completion of the first draft should not signify the end of the matter. Children should be encouraged to read their first draft and, in discussion with the teacher or other pupils, try to make further alterations to this first draft. It is not so much

Figure 3.2   *What happened next?*

a matter of improving upon what they have written, it is more a case of developing a habit of reading and revising a text as would an adult author. The immediate results may not be spectacular but the gradual acquisition of the habit of redrafting will be invaluable at a later stage in the development of a skilled writer.

Eventually, in the junior school, children will be helped and encouraged through reflection to consider goals other than global ones; for example, to emphasise a point, to stress the atmosphere, to subtly convey a message, to indicate sympathy or annoyance in their writing. This will increase children's sensitivity to texts both as readers and writers.

Furthermore, in the later stages of the primary school, there is a highly specific way in which co-operation between teacher and child can be directed towards improving a child's written language. Perera (1984) points out that beyond the age of eight children become more adept at employing subordinate clauses in their writing. Prior to the age of eight subordinate clauses are more prevalent in their speech than in their writing. The reversal of this continues well into the teenage years, which suggests that to enhance this progression in some way would be beneficial.

There are two ways to support and enhance this progression. One is for teachers to play an active role in redrafting the children's written prose, working with each child, or even with small groups of children, and demonstrating how with the use of connectives, pronouns and various features of punctuation, their writing can be amended to achieve increasing fluency. To be effective, this must be done within class at the time of writing rather than afterwards away from the children as a marking exercise for the teacher.

The other way to affect the progression in the use of subordinate clauses is for the children to be continuously experiencing texts, varying in language patterns, being read aloud by the teacher accompanied by that teacher remarking upon, and at times illustrating, the various language patterns. Writing them up on the blackboard or on the overhead projector will be effective.

Advanced composing and advanced reading development

The development of writing ability can be taken a step further, into the realms of 'knowledge-transforming' (Bereiter and Scardamalia 1987), if the readers are subsequently required to use the story that they have just read and transform it into a very different story, say with different characters and with a different ending or action. This, like many other exercises, should be promoted as a workshop group activity in which small groups of pupils read a text and then orally transform it, before each member of the group attempts to make his own written interpretation of the outcome of the discussion. This activity stimulates reflection which is essential to understanding a text, it activates mental cognition in the reformulation of thoughts and of the information one possesses, and it exercises the ability to produce continuous prose with a specific purpose in mind.

There should be a conscious and continuing effort throughout junior classes to include in the teaching programme practice in various forms of writing ranging from personal narrative to impersonal non-narrative writing. These will include imaginative stories in which the children themselves are included; repeating stories that have been read to them or that they have read; describing happenings, events and even objects in some detail; writing up accounts of experiments in science and design technology; writing letters to friends and in response to advertisements; writing as though through the eyes of another person; writing critiques of actions by other children and of events in their neighbourhood; and attempting to write in poetic form.

Furthermore, the old idea of a project should not be ignored. If planned and executed with care then reporting on a science experiment or completing a geographical or historical project can be an intensive and purposeful exercise in thinking, reading, writing and decision making. 'Thinking and decision making' will be exercised in group discussions concerning sources, selection of material, identification of audience, presentation and allocation of tasks. 'Reading' will involve searching for and selecting relevant information, whilst 'writing' will involve the composition of texts to suit particular and specific purposes.

At its best this type of work is an excellent training in research, whether it be reporting an activity such as a science experiment or something that has happened in the past or in another part of the world. It does, however, require conscientious teaching and meticulous attention to detail. Too many projects in the past were allowed to flounder because of insufficient input by teachers. Not only should teachers guide children towards the materials to be read, they must become seriously involved in the discussions referred to above, allowing initiative on the part of the children, yet challenging them to reread, rewrite and rethink on many occasions, all of which will encourage development in the ability to use spoken language with increasing skill and effect. Incidentally, this should not be equated with 'teacher prescription of ways of talking' (Phillips, 1985). Rather, the children should be guided as to what should be discussed rather than told how to discuss things. Out of this, over a period of time and with much practice, children will develop a disposition to quickly adopt the appropriate genre of discourse for the task in hand. This process of development will affect their progress in choosing the appropriate genre in writing and it will provide them with the ability to appreciate the genre of texts which they read.

Further discussion and guidance can be found in Wray and Lewis (1997) in which they describe their research into 'Extending Interactions with Texts'. The model they used, called EXIT, consisted of a sequence of ten procedures that would constitute a classroom project. These can be interpreted as follows and make a useful checklist for any teacher engaging in project work:

1 Elicitation of previous knowledge already held by the learner.
2 Establishing purposes and deciding what is needed to extend knowledge.
3 Locating information: identifying possible sources.
4 Adopting an appropriate way of using the material collected.
5 Interacting with the texts: reading and studying the texts in order to comprehend them fully.
6 Monitoring understanding: resolving difficulties in comprehension.
7 Sifting and recording information.
8 Evaluating the information in terms of its authenticity.
9 Adopting strategies to retain the information in the memory.
10 Matching the form of reportage to the audience.

Roughly speaking this model falls into three sections, preparation, reading and follow up, and corresponds to Whitehead's cyclic process of learning: romance, precision, and generalisation.

In discussing the implementation of the model, Wray and Lewis give a full description of activities and teaching strategies that were employed at every stage in the model. These included:

• preparatory work such as brainstorming, questioning, identifying sources and discussing ways of collecting the information required;
• working on texts through DARTs activities, which include cloze procedure, prediction exercises and sequencing which have been adapted to the needs and abilities of children at Key Stage 2 level, and which were considered by Lunzer and Gardner (1979) to be helpful in developing comprehension of texts;
• modelling and marking the texts to illuminate information, followed by discussion of what has been noted and marked;
• reviewing and if necessary re-ordering what has been learned or encountered;
• recording or passing on the information in writing, using an appropriate style and arrangement of text.

Each of these groups of activities, signifying the various stages in a project, is dealt with discretely. For example, the actual reading of texts is underpinned by DARTs exercises so that children acquire the ability and the habit of 'working at a text' and not merely reading uncritically.

Naturally, it is the activities that are the basis of the EXIT model, but their impact on children will be greatly reduced if little thought is given to the teaching techniques and strategies that are described in Chapter 3 of *Extending Literacy* (Wray and Lewis, 1997), and also to those implicit in the Whitehead cyclic model of teaching referred to earlier.

More advanced word study

One of the major aims during the junior school years, in classes Y3, Y4, Y5 and Y6, should be to build up the widest possible vocabulary of automatically recognised words. Upon this depends largely whether or not children will become effective and committed readers. Opportunities for this arise in various activities, amongst them:

1 through challenging children to rewrite a story incorporating unusual words. Teach them how to use a thesaurus as soon as possible and set this activity up as a group collaborative exercise, whereby a group see how far they can amend each other's text;
2 similarly, working on a group basis, initiate a search for as many words as possible relating to a theme or action – a kind of buzz session but with the added help of a dictionary and thesaurus;
3 through short but intensive sessions with a small group of children at a time, search for evidence of the affects of prefixes and suffixes on the meaning of words, and for examples of pronunciation idiosyncrasies – where the spelling carries the meaning such words as *nation, national, know, knowledge, medic, medicine, medical, medicinal* and where there is a foreign derivation as in *envelope* and *cafe*;
4 through reading poems and other literary texts on subjects similar to or the same as those upon which the children are writing, note and discuss how the poet or author uses words.

These are all useful activities in calling attention to words, but to be effective in the long term there must be a conscious effort to provide revision in order to reinforce the learning that has taken place.

Rectifying earlier failures in reading

If you are faced with older children who cannot read or can read only with difficulty, do not start initially with a single method. Try to explore the problem facing each child individually as a preliminary study to seeing how that child sees print and how reading behaviour is regarded. Ask the child to attempt to read a simple statement written by you and concerning something of particular interest to that child. From this try to discern what it is that is causing difficulty. Does the child know some words and not others? What is it about those words that causes difficulty? Can a start be made with the initial sounds of words? If not help is needed with the identification of individual letter sounds. However, in many cases the problem will be connected with vowels, digraphs and with splitting the word up into pronounceable segments, and this may be caused by the child not being able to respond automatically to particular letter strings. Show the child what segments you see in the word and get the child to memorise them. Ask the child to write about something of interest – not a long piece, perhaps simply a word or phrase. If this is wrongly written show how you would write it and try to explain why you would write it that way. From this try to build up with the pupil a number of words about things which the child considers important. Usually the problem does not lie in not knowing the sounds of letters but in the trick of seeing patterns of letters, such as *bi-cy-cle, en-gine, bl-ock, bu-ster* or *bus-ter*, which will help the reader to cope with the variable sounds of vowels and digraphs and blends.

Therefore the teacher's task is a dual one: the child must be taught responses to letter clusters in words, and must be encouraged to experiment in responding to those clusters and in attempting to combine them into a complete response to the word.

There is a third task for the teacher which is to see that the words that the child encounters in this way are repeatedly recalled at frequent intervals for at least a week after each encounter.

When work of this nature has been established, it is then advisable to combine reading, spelling and writing implying the approach used by Fernald and referred to in Chapter 2 in the section on *Reading for slow learners* on page 38. This method, acting as a 'crash programme', will help the children to begin to regard words in their context and to see them as part of the sentence patterns of language. From this they will be helped in the search for meaning. They will begin to realise words are part of a meaningful statement and they will therefore begin to search for meaning rather than passively expecting meaning to emerge. Just as with children who learn to read normally, the slow learner must learn, albeit at a slower pace, how to use a variety of cues in order to build up a meaningful response to a text. This takes time and patience and it must not be allowed to become tedious.

Summary of critical points of awareness in learning to read, spell and write

1 In learning to read:
   a that words can be matched to what is spoken or thought
   b that letters indicate sounds
   c that letter clusters, especially onsets and rimes, are the elements to look for in words
   d that strings of words must be reflected upon in order to deduce meaning
   e that syntactic and semantic constraints make written language highly predictable.

2 In learning to spell:
   a that words can be segmented in relation to sound
   b that the segments (strings of letters, onsets and rimes) have a highly predictable relationship occurring in many different words, so that analogies can be drawn between words
   c that spelling follows pronunciation within certain broad limits and that inconsistencies are not entirely random
   d that relationships in meaning are indicated in the spelling in many cases.

3 In learning to compose a text:
   a that thoughts can be transcribed
   b that thoughts can be represented by words, although a word may suggest a series of thoughts
   c that writing prose requires an accepted form and tends to contain more detail than speech
   d that punctuation signs supplement the form of the text and contribute to its meaning.

4 In learning to write physically:
   a that there is a correct starting point for each letter in its pure form
   b that there is a correct sequence in forming each letter
   c that discrete letters must be joined for optimum fluency
   d that a few letters take on a different formation in order to achieve this fluency in cursive writing.

In following the above programme teachers will be aware that, as stated earlier, many items overlap and that their placement and duration depend upon the experiences and abilities of the children. In fact it is the interweaving of the teaching of reading, writing and spelling that helps children to acquire these complex skills. They will also appreciate the important role of oral language at all stages in facilitating effective teaching and learning. During the time that they are learning to read, spell and write children are experiencing new language structures which they get from the stories they hear and read and which they develop through oral and written activities, hence the importance that must be attached to practice in oral communication and to reading aloud both stories and poetry to children.

Finally, it is important to remember that young children only concentrate when interested and involved and then only for a few minutes at a time. So keep everything short and remember the value of repetition, revision and the resulting reinforcement of learning.

Once a day is a recipe for failure! Time allowed for forgetting can be as influential to the results as time given to teaching.

There are therefore dangers in the literacy hour if it is regarded as the only period of the day when matters concerned with English – reading, writing, spelling – are dealt with. Within the literacy hour itself there is ample room for variety, but it should be accompanied by attention to development in the use of English during other periods of the day. Reading and writing activities connected with history, geography, numeracy and science should be seen as part of the literacy programme at Key Stage 2. These subjects provide a context for learning to use new words and language patterns in an interesting and purposeful way. In particular they provide an appropriate vehicle for the development and understanding of impersonal non-narrative writing that is so pertinent to an ability to read and write informative reports of a factual nature.

4 Pitfalls with phonics

Very few subjects of the curriculum carry with them the danger of being misinterpreted . Unfortunately, reading is one of them. People who would otherwise be regarded as thoughtful have been known to conclude rashly that reading is a summative process in which phonemes are joined in a simplistic way by children who have learned their alphabet. This is patently not so and no teacher would base teaching upon such a naive approach. Nevertheless, because the majority of teachers experienced no undue difficulties in learning to read, there can arise the danger of over-optimistic assumptions being made about children's abilities to cope with the intricacies of learning to read. For example, it is easy to assume that children have an innate ability to 'split words up' in the desired way and then to blend the parts together. Likewise, it is easy to assume that children are always thinking of the message when they are reading. Such optimism is based on careless assumptions and should be guarded against.

It would seem wise, therefore, to clarify the undoubted pitfalls of assumptions that can easily be made in the welter of activity surrounding very young children. They are:

1 to assume that children readily understand the correspondence between grapheme and phoneme. It takes time for them to see and to understand that letters have a specific form and that sounds can be attached to letters. These are abstract concepts, the significance of which only becomes evident in the context of words, and then only gradually after many relevant experiences with letters and words;

2 to assume that children readily acquire the knowledge that some graphemes have more than one sound, *a* in *hat* and *hate*, and that some phonemes have more than one grapheme, /s/ in *side* and *city*.

A skilled reader automatically and instantaneously adjusts to these anomalies, but someone who is in the early stages of learning to read has to learn to make qualifying adjustments to possibly inappropriate first responses.

For example, in approaching the word *cure* phoneme by phoneme, unless the initial /k/ is severely clipped, which is difficult for an adult, more so for a child, then the response becomes /ker/. This followed by (∂:) or even the more appropriate /jew/ (as in fe*w*) can be misleading unless children are taught and encouraged to be flexible and, in this case, to change or modify the attempt at the initial phoneme. Adaptive searching behaviour of this kind requires courage based on confidence to make such adjustments. Therefore, the teacher's task is to be both supportive and helpful when a child is faced with this kind of dilemma. Encouragement is not enough; help is essential to avoid failure;

3 to assume that the identification of a word is merely a matter of summation of the individual phonemes represented by all the individual graphemes with minor adjustments in the sounding out process where necessary. Virtually from the outset the young learner will come face to face with blends, such as *bl, br, str, scr, ld, nd, ng* in words such as *blow, bread, string, scratch, cold,* and *sing*. The sooner the child is taught to treat these blends as single sounds separate from the two or three phonemes of which they are compiled, the easier will be the task of identifying and reading aloud the words in which they are found. Furthermore, it will not be long before silent letters appear in words like *gnome, know, light, school, scissors*. Again these can more easily be remembered in comparison with other words in comparable groups rather than in isolation: *gnome, gnat, gnaw, gnash; know, knob, knock, knife, knee, knave, knight, knit, knot; light, might, right, fight; school, scholar, schooner, scheme; scissors, scientist;*

4 to assume that children have an automatically triggered, innate ability to blend phonemes, blends, digraphs, syllables and morphemes together in order to form words. Children need to be taught how to do this. They must be shown how to do it by the teacher demonstrating orally and with accompanying written segments of words and be given practice in doing it themselves;

5 to assume that morphemic and syllabic boundaries are readily identified in words. One of the great advantages of adopting the ideas on rhyming and alliteration advanced by Goswami is that distinguishing between the onset and the rime in a word provides the teacher with a device for showing children, over time and by using scores of instances, how to set about segmenting words into pronounceable parts which retain the overall sound of the words. Thus *light* becomes /l/, /ait/ rather

than /l/, /i/, /g/, /h/, /t/, or any other misleading combination of sounds, and can be compared visually and orally with *fight, right, sight, might*;

6 to assume that children, having identified the rimes in words, can immediately pronounce the words with fluency, clarity and assurance. Monosyllabic words may not provide a problem, but natural blending of polysyllabic words can pose quite a problem for the learner in the early stages. Therefore, practice in blending onset with rime in monosyllabic words is necessary to establish a correct form of response. This demands a further adaption by the learner, from identification of onset separated from rime (*t-able*) to initial consonant or blend joined to vowel or digraph followed by the final consonant or consonant cluster (*ta-ble*), in order to achieve a more flowing blend of the word. Gradually, progression can be made to polysyllabic words, starting with those which are made up from two familiar words, such as *playtime, playmate, penknife, carphone*;

7 to assume that all children readily adopt a searching strategy when responding orally to graphemes, digraphs, syllables, morphemes and letter strings of various forms. Children need to be taught to experiment in their reactions to unfamiliar words. This can be done most effectively when the child feels impelled to resolve the meaning of the text before him or her. That is to say, training in the adoption and application of searching behaviour is best done when unfamiliar words are confronted in a prose or poetic context rather than in isolation. The meaning suggested by the text will provide substance for the attempts at word recognition. This will have a twofold effect. It will encourage the child's efforts whilst at the same time inculcating the type of behaviour that is a necessary requisite of skilled reading, and when the word is successfully identified it should be noted and retained by both teacher and child for subsequent reinforcement and practice.

This last point reminds us of the dangers of a naive reliance upon phonics alone to solve the problems of teaching children to read. Context plays an important part in reading. Expertise in the interpretation of the phono-graphemic cues will not help a reader to understand the meaning of the sentence, *The boy bit the dog*, which has the identical words and letters to *The dog bit the boy*, if the reader is not using syntactic (grammatical) cues and semantic (meaningful) cues. Therefore training in the use of all three types of cues – phono-graphemic, syntactic and semantic – simultaneously on every possible occasion must take place from the earliest stages. Amongst other things this means children must be trained to ask themselves, 'Does it make sense?' and 'What does it say?'

An example of an early exercise in this type of comprehensive reading behaviour would be for the teacher to devise an exercise in which the child has to relate phono-graphemic cues to supportive semantic cues. This would involve the production of a tape recording of familiar sounds: a dog barking, a sheep bleating and so on, with a cat, cow, horse, bird and other everyday sounds such as those of a car engine, an aeroplane, a police siren, ice cream chimes, a telephone ringing and so on. In addition there would be a printout stating what the sounds represented:

> *That is a dog barking*
> *That is a car (engine)*

This type of exercise would have several effects on the young learner. It would indicate that print is an alternative form of representing reality: what the child knows (a dog barking) can be represented in print. (This is the reason why print has been referred to as a 'second signalling system'.) At the same time it would indicate to the child the need to search for meaning in the text (e.g. the response could be *That is a car* or *That is a car engine* depending solely upon the text). The fact that each sentence on the cards began with an identical phrase (*that is*) would begin the process of learning to react to common phrases instantaneously, without hesitation and repetitive analysis, and the ease of response to the repetitive phrase would allow more effort to be given to identifying the target word or words.

One point should be made about exercises of this kind. Whilst their completion gives the pupil a certain amount of pleasure, the frequent encouraging responses of the teacher to the child's effort after each response add greatly to that child's growing confidence and satisfaction. In this way, through frequent teacher interjections, exercises of this kind do not fall into the deadening routine of the old-style ineffective written English exercises that fell into disfavour with teachers some years ago.

Conclusions

By clearly defining the pitfalls in this way teachers will be alerted to the dangers regardless of the approach or scheme that they are using. They remind us that the effectiveness of the teaching will depend upon the skill of the teacher in illuminating for the learner the problems that are being faced, providing guidance in their resolution, and in inculcating searching and experimental behaviours on the part of children when confronted with problems. This latter point can be extended into the realms of reflective behaviour. Arguably one of the most important findings of research in Britain was that those children who scored highly in tests of comprehension were those with a disposition to reflect upon what had been read (Lunzer and Gardner, 1979). From this it can be argued that children who are learning to read in the early stages and who fail to reflect upon what they read are denying themselves a significant set of cues in their attempts to read a text.

Furthermore, training in reflection upon what is read is not something for the early stages alone. Throughout Y3, Y4, Y5 and Y6 reflection should be a constant requirement. It will take many forms, amongst them retelling stories; identifying main characters and events; interpreting a message; transposing a story into a play; following written instructions; re-drafting and amending written work; detecting feeling in characters and authors; commenting critically on published stories, instructions or informative writing.

Thus in any literacy period, whether it be of one hour's continuous duration or divided into shorter periods, teachers will be required to play a supportive, illuminating and stimulating role in directly teaching children to read at all levels whilst at the same time allowing time in which the child has opportunities through practice and experimentation to come to terms with what has been learned with the teacher.

Children must be taught to make allowances for the fact that their initial responses or interpretations may not produce the desired outcome and a certain amount of experimentation will be needed in many instances of tentative word and text analysis. Much that is involved in learning to read requires adaptive behaviour, and it is essential, therefore, that teachers remind themselves continuously of the ease with which superficial assumptions can be made when teaching children, with the result that children may be left with knowledge of facts but with no ideas of how to handle those facts, with an ability to read but without sensitive interpretation.

5 The literacy hour: a theoretical basis for its implementation

The proposals for the establishment of an hour per day devoted to the development of literacy should not be regarded as a retrograde step. It should be seen as an opportunity to regard learning to read as part of a wider development involving the development of cognate abilities in spelling, writing and understanding of language, spoken and written. All of these interact and advancement in one enhances advancement in the others.

Many teachers in the past have combined these aspects of literacy, but the amount of interaction has been variable. It is to be hoped that the new proposals will foster a more determined effort by all teachers to ensure that children are led to understand the implications of each aspect for the others. This in itself will enhance the teaching that is done.

However, it is not merely a matter of mixing up the subjects and crowding in as much information as possible. There must be a framework into which the various aspects of literacy can be fitted, based upon a theory of pedagogy which is easy to implement but effective in outcome. It would be a waste of the concept of the literacy hour to have disparate activities, unconnected to each other, or to spend the whole time on one type of activity, for example, reading activities with no writing or spelling. The former would be confusing to the children and ineffective; the latter would be inappropriate for young active minds.

Hence the question of balance of activities arises: a balance between the active manipulation of materials and apparatus for reading, writing and spelling and a more observational approach to texts, between learning activities and practising those activities, between being told and finding out, between observational learning and active participation in learning. The possibilities can appear bewilderingly numerous, therefore, a model for teaching must be drawn up which encompasses these options in such a way as to make them manageable. It would be purposeless for a teacher to select items for the literacy hour haphazardly. There must be a pattern which takes into consideration the constraints of the subject matter and the nature of children's learning as well as being manageable for the teacher.

Constraints of the subject matter

The subject matter of the literacy hour is communication, the main elements of which are spoken language, reading, writing and spelling. These have all been shown in previous chapters to interact and in so doing to promote development in each.

In learning to spell an insight is gained into the construction of words, the patterns of English spelling and the relationships between sounds and symbols. In learning to write insights are gained into the formation of letters, the form of words and, subsequently, into the composition of texts. Underlying all of this, the effective use of spoken language, especially in the universalistic sense of Bernstein's codes, enables the learner to appreciate with greater ease the patterns of written language in the form of texts. Indeed speech, spelling and writing can be construed as the constructive side of written language. From them texts are composed which means that by engaging in these constructive activities children are gaining insights into the requirements of skilled reading.

This is fortunate in terms of the variety of activity that can be provided during the literacy hour. It means that reading, writing and spelling can be regarded as interconnected elements of one comprehensive development – the development of literacy. Furthermore, they can be made to impinge more closely upon one another and so promote each other more intensively than was possible when they were treated as separate subjects on the timetable.

For example, discussion can be followed by reading connected with the discussion, followed by word study and spelling involving precise teaching. This, in turn, can be followed by writing, using what has just been learned, followed by further precise teaching, further practice in rereading and redrafting and some form of plenary discussion calling attention to what has been learned. Such variety within the space of an hour is a tremendous advance upon the old idea of a separate reading lesson or a writing lesson or a spelling lesson.

The nature of children's learning

In discussing what children can learn most readily during the early stages, it is easy to forget the limitations imposed by their inability to concentrate for long periods of time, especially when dealing with difficult and seemingly intractable material. Anyone who has taught children to read, and especially children who do not find it easy, knows that the concentration span can be so short it can be measured in minutes and, what is more, it decreases significantly as time passes. However, it is usually true to say that the intensity of concentration correlates highly with the degree of active participation on the part of the learner. Mental participation alone during these early stages, when dealing with the rather abstract aspects of word identification, can impose an undue strain on young children, if not accompanied by opportunities to engage actively in the manipulation and 'handling' of words. For example, seeing the letters of the word *cat* written and being expected to remember their sequence will be less compelling than being expected to arrange wooden cut-out letters in a sequence that forms the word *cat*. Furthermore, the handling and manipulation of the letters engages the tactile and kinaesthetic senses of the child, which adds to the sensory input through the eyes, making the act of learning more intense.

These arguments suggest short periods of precision teaching, where something precise is taught and learned in such a way as to give the learner a reasonable chance of retaining it in the long-term memory. The old idea of telling a child what an unknown word was and, without any additional attention, expecting the child to remember that word was unrealistic.

Obviously concentrated learning periods cannot last too long: ten or fifteen minutes at the most, and in many circumstances two or three minutes may be all that is appropriate.

Naturally, these short periods of intense precision teaching and learning will be followed by practice exercises or tasks that involve the new learning plus some reflection. It is such sequences that form the basis of the teaching notes in the Teacher's Guide to Goswami's reading scheme, *Rhyme and Analogy* published by `Oxford University Press as part of the Oxford *Reading Tree* scheme. Here one finds words, onsets, rimes, syllables and letter strings to be learned from words incorporated in rhyming story books. Exercises and games using these words are described in detail.

These suggestions by Goswami provide teachers with a formidable collection of activities concerned with teaching the details of word recognition and reading skills. However, teachers should not be misled into thinking that this is sufficient. Other factors must be incorporated into the teaching cycle in order to ensure continued involvement by the learner, a sustained effort to retain what has been learned and confirmation that what has been learned can be recalled after a period of time.

This suggests that the learner needs motivating, and on many occasions will need re-stimulating repeatedly during the lesson. Learning is seldom easy and young learners, or learners of any age who are finding difficulty in learning, frequently lose the incentive to learn and require some action by the teacher that will re-motivate them and enable them to maintain their concentration until the task has been completed. Many reading schemes provide attractively illustrated books but focusing on the illustrations is inadequate in itself for the purpose. Looking at attractive pictures is not the real objective. The objective is to get the children to realise that it is the written text that is essential in conveying the full enjoyment of the books, the illustrations are merely supportive; and children should be helped to realise this from the outset. Discussions centred on the book to be read or even the tasks to be accomplished – for example, learning the alphabet – should always precede the activity. Speculation regarding such aspects of the text as the form of letters, or about where or when certain words have been met, or about the possible contents of a book: these informal introductory approaches to the lesson will stimulate interest and help the children to centre their minds upon the task in hand.

As the teaching proceeds it is important to keep in mind the fact that relevant motivational remarks by the teacher are an important ingredient in the learning process. They help to bolster the confidence of the learner in a supportive way, and they can help to lighten an otherwise tedious piece of learning. It is amazing how widespread the notion is that all learning is exciting and engrossing, when much of it can be bewilderingly difficult for many children. Therefore, whenever possible teachers should endeavour to make supportive and encouraging suggestions.

Another way of motivating and inspiring or urging children to learn is by questioning them as the learning session proceeds. The Literacy Task Force in its publication, *The Implementation of the National Literacy Strategy* (1997), refers to 'high frequency questioning (especially with challenge) and frequent provision of feedback' as general factors which characterise effective teaching. This characteristic needs further examination, because the ability of teachers to ask thought-provoking questions appears from various research exercises to be lacking amongst all but the most effective teachers.

Many teachers appear to be satisfied with simplistic questions that merely require a restatement of what the learner has just been told, without the learner being challenged to use this newly acquired knowledge and to relate it to other knowledge. For example, when reading, a child who stumbles over a word is frequently told the word and then asked to repeat it, whereas a more challenging approach would be to ask the child questions which cause him to work out for himself a response to the word.

Beyond the early stages of learning to read this deficiency in questioning techniques takes a similar form. Many comprehension exercises require little reflection upon what has been read and no deductive or inductive thinking is necessary. All that is required is a repetition of factual statements taken directly from the text. Hence, children are not encouraged to adopt a pro-active approach to reading. This criticism applies equally to the questions that are posed in history and geography lessons. Often what is required is simply a repetition of facts, whereas one of the advantages of having history and geography as curriculum subjects in primary schools is that they provide excellent opportunities for evaluative reading from which conclusions, which are not stated in the text, may be drawn. Not only are the teacher's questions crucial in developing this form of discriminatory reading, the children must be encouraged and trained to pose questions of this nature. Equally, critical reading of poetry and prose requires training in answering and posing questions concerning feelings and reactions which in themselves are frequently ephemeral and, therefore, easily treated lightly.

The important place of questioning rests more upon its use as a thought-provoking instrument than as a checking device. Naturally, it has its place as the latter, but its real potency as a teaching device is to ensure that children learn to think about what they have learned and to make decisions for themselves using what has been learned. For example, having taught a child one of the sub-skills of reading, such as the interrupted digraph *a-e* in the word *cake*, questions should provoke thought about other words containing *a-e*. Although care has to be taken not to dissipate the young learner's thoughts by requiring too many examples, to dwell solely upon one instance of *a-e* in a word increases the difficulty of memorising that particular word and misses the opportunity to foster understanding of the concept behind the interrupted digraph in English.

Throughout the primary school years teachers should keep in mind the fact that understanding by young children of some aspect of the spelling or grammatical systems of English does not necessarily equal an ability by those children to explain those aspects but merely to use them. This again will severely constrain the formulation of questions. Frequently teachers will require examples rather than explanations in answer to questions.

The cyclic process of teaching

In the above remarks about the part to be played by the teacher in meeting the needs of children can be seen the beginnings of a cyclic process in teaching, whereby the teacher follows a pattern of motivating the learner, teaching the learner and interjecting re-motivational comments and guidance whilst the teaching proceeds. To complete the cycle, the teacher provides the opportunity to practise what has been learned, either in the form of exercises or in the form of reading or writing which involves using the new knowledge or skill that has been gained. This is a basic form of an adaptation of Whitehead's cyclic process of learning, consisting of romance, precision and generalisation.

However, a further cycle in the teaching and learning process can be introduced to encompass reinforcement and recall of what has been learned. This cycle will involve renewed motivation, which may take the form of questions concerned with what has been learned or of general comments of encouragement by the teacher. Reinforcement requires some repetition of the learning that has taken place previously although more imaginatively, the matter to be revised will be couched in a different form so that interest is re-motivated and a fresh perspective gained. Recall is involved in reworking the subject matter and in response to the assessment that is necessary to ensure that the learning has been successful. This can be further extended into a secondary stage of generalisation, where the newly acquired learning is associated with or incorporated into previously held skills.

A good example of this complete cyclic process would be where the teacher wished to introduce words containing the digraph *ee*. The children would be asked if they knew a nursery rhyme about a sheep. *Baa baa Blacksheep* would then be introduced and read by the teacher. A copy could be illuminated on the overhead projector and the lesson would be concerned with identifying words containing the digraph *ee*. These words could then be finger-traced on cards, constructed from wooden cut-out letters, overwritten and, possibly, copied by the children. The more adventurous and more able children may be encouraged to attempt to write the words without copying. This precision stage would be followed by groups and individuals attempting to identify the words with *ee* in the nursery rhyme itself and by all reading the poem together.

This would take up at least a quarter of the literacy hour and it would then be time to move to another form of activity. Much would depend upon the mood of the class and only a teacher can assess what form of activity should follow. It could take the form of drawing and labelling sheep. It could consist of searching for other words, elsewhere, which contain *ee*. It could consist of exploratory writing connected with the nursery rhyme and involving inventive spelling. Or it could be silently looking at or re-reading previously studied texts and raising points for discussion with the teacher.

With the above aspects of the lesson being conducted on a whole-class or large group basis, the organisation of the class could then move quite naturally to a small group or a small group plus individual form. This would allow the teacher to do further work with a small group of those children who had not fully understood the work so far whilst those who had grasped the function of the digraph *ee* could be set to work individually reading or composing and writing texts which contain *ee* words and other words containing previously learned digraphs, such as *ea* or *oo* for example.

Having completed *approximately* fifteen to twenty minutes on small-group and individual activities, and in which the teacher should feel free to spend a little time at least with individuals and groups other than the targeted group, the class can reassemble as a whole for a plenary session in which the new learning can be revised and any additional work by individuals noted. The important thing to remember is that after the passage of a period of time, preferably still within the same literacy hour in which the children learned about *ee* words from the nursery rhyme, they should be reintroduced to the poem, and the words containing *ee* recalled. This should be done as a simple way of reinforcing the initial learning, and it should be repeated at various intervals over the following weeks to ensure that the words and the concept of the digraph *ee* have been thoroughly learned, internalised and generalised, so that whenever the children meet *ee* words in their future reading they will be able to relate to them at least, if not recall them immediately. In this way the cycle of learning continues and the new learning is integrated into other learning.

At a later stage in the primary school an example of the cyclic process can be seen when the teacher's aim is to enable pupils to appreciate two different kinds of descriptive writing: one describing a joyful event, the other a tragic event. The initial motivational part of the hour should encompass a reading by the teacher of two texts followed by a general discussion about the differences between the two pieces. Then, at the precision stage, the children working in pairs could draw up a list of words and phrases from each text which exemplify joy and tragedy. Samples of these extractions could be offered to the whole class, with the teacher commenting on them and encouraging reactions from the rest of the class. Next, the children could be asked to use the thesaurus to find alternatives to the words that they have chosen and, generalising from what has been learned so far, compose two similar texts using the alternative words. Again a selection of these new texts could be read out to the class for critical evaluation. Having completed this study of words connected with joyful and tragic events, two possibilities for further activities suggest themselves. The children working individually could choose either to write one joyful or tragic piece of prose or two shorter pieces, one joyful, one tragic. They would then gather in groups, read one another's contributions and decide upon the best examples from each group, giving reasons for their choice. This forms a second precision stage within the lesson, which may be followed by a final plenary session in which some general points are made about descriptive writing and the expression of feelings.

The arrangement of this lesson may not fit precisely into the format for lessons proposed in *The National Literacy Strategy: Framework for Teaching* (1998), but it is equally comprehensive in its coverage and it encapsulates the spirit of the governmental suggestions. Furthermore, it is offered as evidence that teachers should not succumb to a universal 'straightjacket' in their teaching. In fact, a more positive attitude would be to regard the *Framework for Teaching* as a basis for inventive initiatives.

This adaptation of the theoretical model of learning provided by Whitehead can serve as a constant reminder to teachers of the importance of their teaching strategies. It can also reassure them that they are covering the ground thoroughly, so that as cycles of teaching evolve, the children will be progressing on the basis not merely of the work covered, but on that of the actual learning that has been accomplished, and proved by recall to have been accomplished.

This on the whole will mean that the literacy hour, whether seen as sixty minutes of continuous work on aspects of literacy or as several periods of time which when added together amount to one hour's work on literacy, will consist on most occasions of inter-connected work.

The need for a programme of learning

One of the weaknesses which has bedevilled the teaching of reading in the past has been the lack of a clearly defined programme of learning that could be systematically followed and referred back to with any degree of confidence. Teachers in Britain did not wish to follow the dictates of a comprehensive teachers' manual. This led to a haphazard approach to revision in British schools. Often teachers did not have the detailed plans of their teaching to which they could refer when considering what to revise. The result was that some aspects of learning to read were revised whilst others were covered only once, which was insufficient to ensure thorough learning. Now, with recent government requirements under the National Curriculum and proposals under the National Literacy Campaign, teachers will already have a basic scheme of work. Naturally, this scheme will have to be adapted to meet the varying needs of children with differing levels of ability and interests. It will not entail much extra effort. Keeping details of progress for each child will provide the teacher with a very clear picture of what each child has done and what, therefore, needs to be revised. Only the naive think that revision is unnecessary. One has only to watch babies learning to put food in their mouths or read how outstanding musicians practise to see how essential it is to practise. Children in school are no different. They need to be motivated to learn, they need precise instruction and guidance and they need practice and additional reinforcement followed by further practice on many occasions. Hence, it should be the aim of teachers to establish a rolling programme of teaching in which new learning is introduced and old learning is periodically revised and revitalised, not once but repeatedly. With this will come success for the child, which in itself is strongly motivational, and when to this is added the teacher's skilful motivational interjections even the most laborious learning will be accomplished satisfactorily.

Hence, the cycle of teaching – motivation, precision teaching, general application or practice – with opportunities within that cycle to regress and reform, to re-motivate, re-teach and give further additional practice wherever necessary, provides a model of teaching that is supportive for the child, refreshing for the teacher, allows comprehensive coverage of the subject matter and provides a 'snowball' effect of learning. Furthermore, it can be applied to the literacy hour as a whole and to its four parts independently as defined in *The National Literacy Strategy: Framework for Teaching* (1998). Taking the four sections of 15, 15, 20 and 10 minutes as numbered 1 to 4, in section 1 the example given of reading a 'big book' to the class would involve a romance or motivational stage where the teacher arouses interest by comments on the impending story and then reads it. The precision stage involves noting words or phrases, punctuation and layout, to be followed by the third stage – generalisation – in which shared reading of the 'big book' takes place. A similar progression applies with shared writing. For example, the teacher may decide to compose and write a story with the whole class using the overhead projector. The romance stage will involve discussion and suggestions, the precision stage will include writing by the teacher together with questions concerning the use of words, capitals and punctuation marks needed to achieve the desired meaning or message, and finally, the stage of generalisation which will involve reading aloud what has been written on the overhead projector.

In section 2 of the literacy hour the romance stage will be brief, merely a reference back to the work in section 1, which now becomes the romance stage for section 2. The real body of work in section 2 in turn becomes a precision stage following the motivational aspect of section 1. At this second section teacher and class concentrate more precisely upon the phonics and grammar that have been noted in the stories encountered in section 1. It is here that specific and pointed teaching takes place. And because the teaching is carried out in some depth, the section should finish with some revision, reinforcement and discussion of what has been learned, thus ending with a short stage of generalisation in the form of a reminder of what has been done.

Section 3 again involves all three stages in the teaching model, but with particular emphasis on the generalisation of the work that has been done in the previous sections, whilst for the targeted group the emphasis is again on the precision stage. In both cases the children will need motivating and re-motivating occasionally and the section should end with an opportunity for personal reflection by each individual upon what has been read or written.

Finally, in section 4 the main emphasis will be on generalising what has been learned. This will involve some surreptitious romance in the form of recapitulation of the essence of what has been done and some further precision in the form of re-encountering some of the details of the lesson, but the main task of the teacher will be to enable the children to appreciate what they have accomplished and hence be prepared to be receptive to further developments in subsequent lessons.

A model such as this adaptation of Whitehead's model of learning, with its cycles within cycles of teaching, could be the dynamic foundation for what could otherwise appear from government documents to be a rigid diktat alien to the inventiveness of the more skilful British teachers.

Similar arguments can be found in Chapter 3 of *Extending Literacy* (Wray and Lewis, 1997) stressing the importance of the actual teaching that is done, whether in the form of direct instruction, thought-provoking or suggestive questioning, supportive participation or specific demonstration and, finally, recapitulation and revision. So much depends upon the quantity and quality of this input by teachers over such a vast area of learning that individual instruction, whilst having its place as a supportive and revisory measure, cannot be regarded as an adequate substitute for group and class teaching as an economical use of the time available.

6 Postscript

Useful word lists

A useful source of common words that have been categorised according to their spelling patterns and from which teachers can draw words for comparison and illustration when teaching children to read and spell has been produced by Dr Joyce Morris in conjunction with the Montessori Centre in London. This list conforms to the three basic spelling patterns of English defined in 1962 by the linguist C. C. Fries. Dr Morris's list, based on her Phonics 44 programme, begins with the spelling pattern consonant-vowel-consonant, listing first words with single consonants: *am, bad* and a list of similar *-a-* words; *bed* and *-e-* words; *if, in, it, bib* and *-i-* words; *on, ox, bod* and *-o-* words; *up, us, bud* and *-u- words;* plus CVC first names such as *Dan* and *Ben*. Still with the CVC pattern, consonant blends, first at the beginning of words such as *blot, clap, flag*, and then at the end of words such as *milk, help, fact, went* and so on, are introduced. This is followed by words beginning and ending with a blend and then by words which end in a double consonant, such as *bell, hill, kiss* and *stuff*. And still with the CVC pattern the consonant digraphs, *-ng, -nk, sh-* and *-sh, ch-* and *-ch*, and finally, the two forms of *-th*. All of these types of word fall into Fries's first set of spelling patterns.

The second set consists of words containing the interrupted digraph or 'magic e', such words as *bake, bike, cone, June*. But intermingled with these words, which Fries considered as a category of their own, Morris introduces the vowel digraphs: *ai, ay, ee, ea* (only the /i:/ sound as in *eat* and *pea*), *ie, y, igh, oa, oe, oo, ue, ew, oo, aw, au, al* (as in ball), *or, ar, ir, ur, er, ou, ow, oi, oy, are* as in *care, air* as in *fair, ear* as in *dear, eer* as in *beer, ere* as in *here, our* as in *tour, oor* as in *poor, ure* as in *cure*.

Parts 2 and 3 of the Morris-Montessori list contain all the variations of multisyllabic words, ranging from *batting* and *wedding* to *physiotherapist, thorough* and *quadrangle*. These are too numerous to mention but they are arranged 'in a sequence which reflects the relative difficulty of sound-symbol correspondences and word structure'.

The main purpose of referring to the list is to suggest that a copy in every school would provide an invaluable resource for teachers. Under no circumstances should it be regarded as a teaching programme.

Another list of words which would be useful for teachers to have would be one which indicates the words most commonly used by young children during the time when they are learning to read, write and spell. This would be especially the case if those were words that were likely to be frequently written or attempted to be written: as Huxford *et al*. (1977) suggested, it might be beneficial to ensure that those words used in an invented form are not allowed to become habitual. As they point out in their paper, 'If children learn to spell words through repeated writing of words' (Peters, 1967; Hornsby, 1984; Lane, 1990 and I might add Fernald, 1943) 'then they presumably can learn incorrect spellings in the same way'.

This is a crucial point to keep in mind when children are using invented spellings. Therefore it is worth giving the list of the 100 commonest words which Huxford and her colleagues arrived at through their examination of 1,254 pieces of writing: 255 by 4-year-olds, 503 by 5-year-olds and 496 by 6-year-olds. As they point out almost all the 'writing' by 4-year-olds in their study had been transcribed in some way by the teachers. In other words the 'writing' consisted of words that the children would have used had they been able to write, although 'in about half the pieces of writing the child had "had a go" at writing'.

The 100 words common to the children of all three ages

and	me	when	can	dog
I	go	put	back	took
the	mum	came	are	liked*
a	some	out	so	come
my	his	you	see	this*
to	home	were	will	called
went	have	him	day	them
he	there	friend*	has	into
was	played*	saw	about	would
in	play	bed	away*	good
it	at	am*	off	outside*
on	dad	down	school	been*

got	of	little	not	their
is	up	one	did	children*
with	house	her	do	ball*
we	for	made	an	girl*
they	she	playing*	that	over*
then	going	but	ran	doing*
like	said	all	time	our
had	because	get	big	baby*

* words not on Reid's (1989) 7-year-old list of 100 most frequent words

Whilst it is not suggested that teachers use this list as a set of words to be taught in isolation, it would be wise to look out for them in the children's written compositions, and ensure that the correct spellings are put before the children at the time of their use; then, depending upon the age of each particular child, an appropriate amount of instruction should be given.

Huxford's list can be compared with List 1 in *The National Literacy Strategy: Framework for Teaching* (1998). This list is unattributed to any research on which it may be based. Presumably it has been collected from children's literature and it consists of 'high frequency words' which 'usually play an important part in holding together the general coherence of texts'. Consequently, there are very few nouns in approximately 150 words.

For children to become familiar with words in a contextual setting will be of great advantage to the young reader. As the government document suggests, knowledge of these words and familiarity with them in a grammatical context will greatly enhance fluency in reading and also contribute to written composition. However, in encountering and appreciating these words it will be necessary for children to know words that are being held together by the listed words. Therefore, it will be necessary for teachers to construct an additional list of nouns which includes those which appear in Huxford's list: common words such as *television, telephone, radio, aeroplane, bicycle, birthday, computer, football, tennis, postman, policeman*; and a correspondingly short list taken from the books that the children will encounter during the literacy hours. These words can then be used alongside the words from List 1 in the government publication, studied in the normal course of shared and guided reading, and used in shared, guided and individual writing to reinforce the original learning. The latter activity will ensure that the list of words from the government publication is used in a variety of contexts.

7 Handwriting: starting points and sequences

There are two generally accepted approaches to the early stages of handwriting. One deals first with letters more or less as they are printed in books:

a b c d e f g h...

Later, when transfer to joined-up writing is imminent, children are shown how to adapt the formation of letters in order to achieve a cursive style, with or without loops on ascenders and descenders:

abcdefghijklmnopqrstuvwxyz

or

abcdefghijklmnopqrstuvwxyz

This approach is slightly less confusing to the absolute beginner, because there is a close conformity between the print that learners see and the shapes they are expected to make when learning to form the letters of the alphabet. It does, however, require a more determined effort when transferring to a cursive style.

In the other approach, children from the beginning are taught to formulate the letters with an entry and an exit stroke:

a b c d e f g h i j k l...

or

abcdefghijkl...

These letters do not match the letter formation used in books and may be somewhat distracting to beginners. However, once learnt this approach makes transfer to joined-up writing almost natural. A little instruction may be necessary, but with most children it will develop naturally from their earlier training.

Letter formation in approach number one

a starting at two o'clock, round anticlockwise and down

b down the ascender, up and round clockwise

c round anticlockwise

d starting at two o'clock, round anticlockwise, up and down

e round anticlockwise

f anticlockwise over and down, lift and cross, soon to be changed to a cursive style: *f f*

g starting at two o'clock anticlockwise and down

h down the ascender and clockwise

i down and dot

j down and dot

k down the ascender, up obliquely to right, lift and down obliquely, soon to be changed to a cursive style: *k k*

l down

m down, up and over twice

n down, up and over

o start at top and proceed anticlockwise

p down the descender, up and round clockwise

q starting at two o'clock, anticlockwise and down the descender

r down, up and over clockwise

s starting at two o'clock, anticlockwise and clockwise, soon to be changed to cursive style: *♂ ♅*

t down the ascender, lift and cross

u down anticlockwise, round, up and down

v starting at eleven o'clock down and up

w as for v twice

x starting at ten o'clock, down obliquely, lift and cross, soon to be changed to cursive style: *x x*

y starting at ten o'clock obliquely across, lift and down descender, soon to be changed to cursive style: *y y*

z left to right, oblique right to left and left to right, soon to be changed to cursive style: *z z*

Letter formation in approach number two

Here the starting or entry points are from the base line:

a b c

with the exit points varying according to the letters:

a b c d e f

At transfer to joined-up writing some adjustment will be required to the levels of entry according to the preceding letter. For example:

man ban cot for cup rubbish

man ban cot for cup rubbish

Further reading

For more detail on the issues raised in this book:

Roberts, G. R. (1989) *Teaching Children to Read and Write*. Oxford: Blackwell Education.

Beard, R. (ed.) (1993) *Teaching Literacy Balancing Aspects*. London: Hodder and Stoughton.

(These two books, together with Adams (1992) and Perera (1984), both referred to below, should be regarded as essential reading for all who aspire to leadership roles in the teaching of reading.)

Beard, R. (ed.) (1995) *Rhyme, Reading and Writing*. London: Hodder and Stoughton.

For comprehensive and readable analyses of research in the United States of America:

Adams, M. J. (1992) *Beginning to Read: Thinking and Learning about Print*. London: MIT Press.

Gibson, E. J. and Levin, H. (1975) *The Psychology of Reading*. Cambridge, Mass: MIT Press.

For analyses of classroom language and its promotion:

Perera, K. (1984) *Children's Writing and Reading: Analysing Classroom Language*. Oxford: Blackwell.

Phillips, T. (1985) Beyond lip-service: discourse development after the age of nine. In G. Wells and J. Nicholls *Language and Learning: An International Perspective*. London: Falmer Press.

Tann, S. (1991) *Developing Language in the Primary Classroom*. London: Cassell. (This book deals with all aspects of English in the National Curriculum.)

Wells, C. G. (1987) *The Meaning Makers: Children Learning Language and Using Language to Learn*. London: Hodder and Stoughton.

For guidance on teaching pupils about language:

Perera, K. (1987) *Understanding Language*. National Association of Advisers in English. (Copies from NATE, Birley School Annexe, Fox Lane Site, Frecheville, Sheffield, S12 4WY, price £1.50 inc. p. and p.)

For detailed suggestions for extending literacy at Key Stage 2:

Pumfrey, P. (1991) *Improving Children's Reading in the Junior School.* London: Cassell.

Wray, D. and Lewis, M. (1997) *Extending Literacy: Children Reading and Writing Non-fiction.* London: Routledge.

For reading schemes closely associated with the literacy hour:

Literacy Links Plus, published by Kingscourt (P.O. Box 1427, London W6 9JS, Tel: 0181-741 2533).

Rhyme and Analogy published as an additional section of the *Reading Tree* scheme by Oxford University Press (Tel: 01536-741519).

(The former links writing, spelling and word study with an extensive range of books for shared and guided reading. The latter covers an approach to word study similar to that which is proposed in this book. Both schemes provide extensive suggestions for work that can be done during the literacy hour.)

For detailed suggestions concerning the contents of the literacy hour:

Iverson, S. and Reeder, T. (1998) *Organizing for a Literacy Hour*, London: Kingscourt.

For suggested aids to teaching and categorised word lists that can be used to illustrate aspects of word analysis:

Hughes, J. M. (1972) *Phonics and the Teaching of Reading.* London: Evans.

Huxford, L., McGonagle, R. and Warren, S. (1997) Which words? Words which 4 to 6 year old children use in their writing. *Reading*, **31**(3), pp. 16–21.

Morris, J. M. (1990) *The Morris-Montessori Word List.* London: Montessori Centre, 18 Balderton Street, W1Y 1TG.

Reason, R. and Boote, R. (1986) *Learning Difficulties in Reading and Writing: A Teacher's Manual.* Windsor: NFER-Nelson.

For information for teachers on English grammar:

Crystal, D. (1992) *Rediscover Grammar.* Harlow: Longman. (This book is highly recommended for teachers who have not studied English beyond GCSE level.)

For government publications on literacy:

Key Stages 1 and 2 of the National Curriculum (1995). London: HMSO.

English in the National Curriculum (1995). London: HMSO.

The Implementation of the National Literacy Strategy (1997). London: Department for Education and Employment (Tel: 0845-602 2260 for Publications Department).

Framework for Literacy (1998).

The National Literacy Strategy: Framework for Teaching (1998). Department for Education and Employment (Tel: 0845-602 2260).

For further details of a rigorous phonic approach:

Goswami, U. and Kirtley, C. (1996) *Rhyme and Analogy: Teacher's Guide.* Oxford: Oxford University Press.

Morris, J. M. (1984) Focus on Phonics: Phonics 44 for initial literacy in English. *Reading*, **18**(1), pp. 13–24.

For further guidance in listening to children read and in the use of miscue analysis:

Arnold, H. (1982) *Listening to Children Reading.* Sevenoaks: Hodder and Stoughton.

Goodman, K. (1969) Analysis of Oral Reading Miscues: Applied Psycholinguistics. *Reading Research Quarterly*, **1**(3).

Goodman, Y. and Burke, C. (1972) *Reading Miscue Inventory.* New York: Macmillan.

For those interested in literacy difficulties:

Bryant, P. and Bradley, L. (1985) *Children's Reading Problems.* Oxford: Blackwell.

Clay, M. M. (1985) *The Early Detection of Reading Difficulties* (3rd ed.). Auckland: Heinemann Education.

Clay, M. M. (1993) *Reading Recovery: A Guidebook for Teachers in Training.* Auckland: Heinemann Education.

(Information about Reading Recovery can be obtained from Reading Recovery National Network, Institute of Education, 20 Bedford Way, London WC1H 0AL, Tel: 0171-612 6585.)

Cripps, C. and Peters, M. L. (1990) *Catchwords: Ideas for Teaching Spelling. National Curriculum Edition.* London: Harcourt, Brace, Jovanovich.

Fernald, G. M. (1943) *Remedial Techniques in Basic School Subjects.* New York: McGraw-Hill.

Hurry, J. (1996) What is so special about Reading Recovery? *The Curriculum Journal*, **7**(1), pp. 93–108.

Merritt, J. (1972) Reading failure: a re-examination. In V. Southgate, *Literacy at All Levels.* London: Ward Lock.

Pumfrey, P. and Elliott, C. (1990) *Children's Difficulties in Reading, Spelling and Writing.* London: Falmer.

For a significant statement on learning to read and learning to spell:

Clay, M. M. (1991) *Becoming Literate.* Auckland: Heinemann Education.

Fernald, G. M. (1943) *Remedial Techniques in Basic School Subjects.* New York: McGraw-Hill. (Excellent on spelling and on teaching slow learners to read.)

Goswami, U. and Bryant, P. (1990) *Phonological Skills and Learning to Read.* Hove: Lawrence Erlbaum Associates.

Perera, K. (1989) *The Development of Prosodic Features in Children's Oral Reading.* PhD thesis, Manchester. (An important contribution to research on the development of comprehension of text.)

Riley, J. (1996) *The Teaching of Reading.* London: Paul Chapman.

For a seminal statement on written composition:
Bereiter, C. and Scardamalia, M. (1987) *the Psychology of Written Composition*. London: Lawrence Erlbaum Associates.

For further information on an apprenticeship approach:
Waterland, L. (1985) *Read With Me: An Apprenticeship Approach to Reading*. Stroud: Thimble.

For an appraisal of children's literature and as a guide in building a class or school library:
Harrison, C. and Coles, M. (eds) (1993) *The Reading for Real Handbook*. London: Routledge.
Townsend, J. R. (1990) *Written for Children*. London: Bodley Head.

For a source book of rhymes and folk tales:
Langley, J. (1996) *Collins Nursery Treasury*. London: Collins.

For detailed guidance on the skills and conventions of handwriting:
Alston, J. and Taylor, J. (1990) *Handwriting Helpline*. Manchester: Dextral Books.

For ideas on the teaching of poetry:
Brownjohn, S. (1980) *Does It Have to Rhyme?* London: Hodder and Stoughton.
Brownjohn, S. (1982) *What Rhymes with 'Secret'?* London: Hodder and Stoughton.
Brownjohn, S. (1989) *The Ability to Name Cats*. London: Hodder and Stoughton.

For a discussion of the assessment of standards in literacy:
Davies, J. (1998) Standards: The Case of Literacy. In C. Richards and P. H. Taylor *How Shall We School Our Children? Primary Education and Its Future*. London: Falmer.
For those wishing to know more about the formation of family reading groups and about the activities of the United Kingdom Reading Association contact UKRA Office, c/o Warrington Road Primary School, Naylor Road, Widnes, Cheshire, WA8 0BP.

Glossary

Blend two or more consecutive letter-sounds in a word where each retains its separate identity. The sounds may be consonants – such as *bl, ld* – or consonants plus a vowel – such as *mi, gre*. The former is called a consonant blend and the latter a consonant-vowel blend.

Blending pronouncing two or more consecutive letters or groups of letters so that each retains its separate identity, either as means of learning the different blends or of trying to arrive at a correct pronunciation of a whole word.

Digraph two letters which together lose their individual identity and represent a single sound – such as *ch, sh, th, eo, ai*.

Diphthong two vowels pronounced as one sound. Frequently subsumed under the term digraph.

Discourse is used in this book as being synonymous with text, i.e. a group of sentences which have a common topic and formal links between them, but which can take the form of spoken or written language.

Grapheme the various forms by which a letter can be printed – *A, a,* a; *g, g*.

Letter string three or more letters – *str, rst, dge, tion, ous*. In some instances the term letter cluster is used.

Onset consonant sounds which may precede the vowel in a syllable, such as *t* in table.

Phoneme phonemes are the basic sound elements of a language. Each phoneme is actually a family of variants of one speech sound. The phoneme itself is an abstract unit of analysis; what we actually hear in speech is one of the various possible sounds – the sound for *c* varies in *cake* and *caught*.

Phonics a term used to indicate an emphasis on sound-letter correspondences. Its application can take various forms in terms of methods of teaching children to read.

Rime the vowel plus consonant element of a syllable – *able* in *table*.

Semantic cues points to meaning within the text.

Syllable the smallest unit of pronunciation – *able, table, pen-cil*.

Syntactical cues pointers from the grammatical structure.

Syntax the way in which words are arranged to show relationships (Crystal).

The International Phonetic Alphabet

In their essays, many students find it necessary to refer to the sounds of morphemes, some of which do not make up complete words: for example, /sei/ in the word *satiate*. The sound of the first two letters can be depicted graphically as 'sai as in *saint*', 'say as in *say*', 'sei as in *seignor*'. The variety in choice makes this an imprecise way of depicting sounds graphemically and, to avoid confusion, the International Phonetic Association had adopted the following system, which enables the writer to show precisely in written form the sounds to which he or she is referring.

Sound	*As in the following*	*Graphic representation of word*

Vowels (long vowels are indicated by the sign :)

i:	see sea ceiling	si: si:liŋ
i	sit goodness	sit gudnis
e	get	get
æ	man	mæn
a:	calm father farm	ka:m fa:ðə fa:m
ɔ	hot	hɔt
ɔ:	saw	sɔ:
o	obey knob	obei nob
u	book put	buk put
u:	too two	tu:
ʌ	cup pup	kʌp pʌp
ə	ago china	əgou tʃainə
ə:	burn world	bə:n wə:ld

Diphthongs

ei	they day	ðei dei
ou	go know	gou nou
ai	my high	mai hai
au	how bough	hau bau

ɔi	boy	bɔi
iə	here idea	hiə aidiə
ɛə	there fare	ðɛə fɛə
ɔə	more four	mɔə fɔə
uə	tour moor	tuə muə

Semi-vowels

| w | will | wil |
| j | yet | jet |

Consonants

b	bed	bed
d	dog	dog
f	fat	fæt
g	go	gou
h	hat	hæt
k	cow kill quick	kau kil kwik
l	leg	leg
m	man	mæn
n	not bun	not bʌn
p	pen	pen
r	red	red
s	see	si:
t	ten	ten
v	very	veri:
z	zone is	zoun iz

Digraphs

ŋ	singer	siŋə
ʃ	ship mission	ʃip miʃən
tʃ	church	tʃə:tʃ
ʒ	measure	meʒə
dʒ	judge	dʒʌdʒ
θ	thin	θin
ð	then the	ðen ðə

It will be noted that *r* is not sounded and, therefore, not depicted when it appears at the end of a word or when it is followed by another consonant; *far* = /fa:/ and *farm* = /fa:m/. However, the *r* is pronounced and depicted when it appears at the end of a word which is immediately followed by a vowel: *far* away = /far awei/.

In some of the examples that are given above, variations in regional accents will mean that the readers will have to make slight adjustments if the letters are to portray their sounds accurately. In this sense the IPA code is not absolutely foolproof.

Index